David Crosby

Copyright 2013 by David Crosby

All rights reserved. No part of this book may be used or reproduced or transmitted in any manner whatsoever without written permission except in the case of brief quotations embodied in critical articles and reviews. For permission contact author David Crosby via e-mail at david@crosbystills.com.

Printed in the United States of America

ISBN-13: 978-1492989967

ISBN-10: 1492989967

Keeping Us Afloat

A Trip down the Intra Coastal Waterway,
and a Journey Through a Marriage

David Crosby

First Edition

David Crosby

This is a true story of my trip down the Intra Coastal Waterway, from Oxford, Maryland to Sarasota, Florida over a two week period in 1999. It's also the true story of my life from childhood to 2002, and of my marriage and career during that period. I've changed a few names to save embarrassment to those who behaved badly. Any mistakes are my own, although I've tried to stick to the facts.

Thanks to my many early readers for proofreading and suggestions, especially Evelyn, Renate and Ian, who all helped me tremendously. A special thanks to Roberta for encouraging me to restart this book after it had been shelved for many years, and to Marilyn for putting up with proofreading and my struggles with how much to share.

Thank you Captain Rick Hanson and Captain Jerry Chitwood for taking a chance on me as the Captain's Mate on this trip.

This is my story, but I will always be grateful to those who have helped me along the way.

David Crosby

Photos that accompany the book may be viewed online by going to my web site at **www.crosbystills.com** and selecting **The Book** on the main menu. The photos from the ICW trip are organized by chapters on the Sets link of the Photostream, and photos from my life story are by topic.

David Crosby

For my Dad, who taught me the art of storytelling

Chapter One

Thursday, November 11th

As we drove into tiny Oxford on that chilly mid November evening in 1999, I couldn't believe this long awaited adventure was about to begin. This was Maryland, and I was surprised that the quaint houses and small marina full of down east style crabbing boats looked more like my impression of New England. It was five o'clock, just in time to sign the papers that would make Chitwood Charters the new owners of "Waxing Gibbous", a 42 foot Grand Banks Motor Yacht. We parked in front of the Oxford Yacht Agency docks, and Gene Lovitt, owner of the Gibbous, went into the office to find the broker as Captain Rick and I carried our bags down the dock to where the boat was supposed to be.

We looked up and down the docks of the small marina, but it wasn't there.

We went to the office, where Gene was waiting for the broker, John Shanahan, to get off the phone. When he was free Rick asked "Where's the boat?"

"We didn't finish getting it ready until late, but we'll bring it over from the yard in the morning", Shanahan answered.

Captain Rick wasn't thrilled at that, since we had planned to spend the night on the boat doing maintenance and then start the trip at dawn. I was anxious to see the boat, and to spend the first of many nights aboard. This trip was the adventure of a lifetime to me, and I couldn't wait to get started. Rick, a lean 5'10'' with a trim gray beard and a deepwater tan, was serving both as the delivery captain and as the representative from Chitwood Charters in the sale. He sat down with Gene and the broker to wade through the paperwork while I looked around the small office area, plastered with pictures of Grand Banks trawlers plowing their way through the waves, and with brochures and magazines featuring these famous "little ships", as the literature says. My wife Jenny and I had been wanting a Grand Banks for 10 years, and it was easy to imagine that I was the one here signing the papers on our new boat. But this time I was just along for the ride.

The money discussions were getting deep in the office and I felt like an eavesdropper, so I went out to the docks to admire the boats. It was a beautiful scene in the twilight, ten different Grand Banks trawlers bobbing gently in the wake of a passing crab boat returning with a boatload of Maryland Blue crabs. A 42 foot GB Classic sat on one dock, awaiting delivery to its new owner the following day. At more than $600,000., it wasn't going to be in my future any time soon. Grand Banks trawlers are built of very thick fiberglass, and are displacement rather than planing boats. That means they ride low in the water, slowly but smoothly, where a planing boat rides on top of the water, bouncing on the waves for a much faster but rougher ride.

Built by American Marine of Singapore starting in 1963, Grand Banks yachts took the workmanlike styling of a commercial fishing boat and added the luxury interiors of a yacht. Although the company switched from building them of mahogany to using fiberglass in 1973, wood touches are everywhere. The stern is mahogany covered, giving it the look of a painted wooden boat. The decks are teak covered, and the interiors are teak walled and teak parquet floored. All of the built in furniture is teak as well, making it hard to believe the boat itself is not made of wood. The narrow walkways outside the raised pilothouse slope upwards towards the bow, and the bow pulpit. The pulpit, a protruding platform and stainless steel railing inspired by the harpoon platform on the front of whaling ships in the 19th century, is handy for setting the anchor, and contributes to the boats classic lines. Pulpits on boats derive their name from a general resemblance to the raised lecterns used for sermons and readings in many churches.

I'd always loved boats with a traditional look, and they just didn't get any more classic than these trawler style yachts. As I walked further down the pier, I saw on the center dock a new 42 foot Grand Banks Europa, a covered rear deck style that Jenny & I had coveted since it was first introduced a decade ago. We were hoping that by the time we were ready there would be enough used ones on the market to find a "fixer upper" in our price range. For now, I was happy to be along for the ride.

We were picking up the "Waxing Gibbous" and taking it from Oxford to Sarasota, Florida, where Chitwood Charters is based. It was Thursday, with Thanksgiving just two weeks away, and Captain Rick and I both had promised to be home for the holiday meal with our families. With the trip expected to take ten days, we didn't have any time to spare. I was also worried about being away from work that long. As the owner and principal photographer of Crosby Stills, a commercial photography studio based in South Carolina, I hadn't been away from the office so long in the nearly fifteen years we'd been in business. My wife Jenny was minding the store, but I fretted over the potential lost business and the long time away from home.

Married for 25 years, Jenny and I had been apart this long only once before, when her father had been ill in Florida battling cancer. Now we'd be connected only by phone. I'd warned Captain Chitwood that if a huge photography project came up while I was on the trip I might have to fly home along the route to do the work, but I was hoping to complete the journey. It was something I'd only dreamed of, 1,300 miles by boat. As I walked the docks a long way from home, I thought about how our anniversary had brought this about.

It started with great promise. Jenny had wanted to do something special to celebrate our anniversary, something unique and different. We'd considered cruises, but we didn't like crowds. Thought about exotic destinations, but she hated flying. But we'd always loved boats. Big boats. We'd bought our first ski boat when I was 30, and our first little houseboat when I was 36. It was a 28 foot, 32 year old boat with chronic engine problems, but I don't think we ever had more fun with a boat than that one.

Which was too bad, because four months after buying it, my wife had her eye on a bigger one. A 52 foot SeaGoing steel hulled boat, it was another big project, and of course, more money. Jenny never had a problem suggesting I take on a project. It was a nice boat though, and I'd spent the spring redoing the interior and painting the hull while it sat in dry dock as the twin outdrives were rebuilt. We'd enjoyed it and had some wild adventures until two years later, when she spied another project for me, but that's a story for later.

But the boat bug had bitten. Jenny had dreamed of the two of us buying a 42 foot Grand Banks trawler and living aboard. We'd even gone so far as doing a little shopping with a boat broker, looking at boats in Florida, but we couldn't make the math work. My commercial photography business was built around local clients in South Carolina, and it just didn't feel that portable.

Since the Big Trawler remained a fantasy goal, we came up with the idea of chartering one to celebrate our anniversary. It seemed perfect. We found Chitwood Charters, a company in

Sarasota, Florida, with a small fleet of Grand Banks docked at the bayside Hyatt, and made our reservation. We planned a week on their biggest boat to celebrate 25 years together.

The boat was a 48 foot wooden trawler, a beautiful teak decked mahogany hull with lines reminiscent of an old sailing ship. Since I had years of experience piloting 52 foot steel hulled houseboats, I told them we wouldn't need a captain. Jenny and I wanted privacy to celebrate our togetherness, and of course, I was hoping that the boat and a few bottles of wine would kick start our love life. At 5' 1" with long brown hair, Jenny had always battled her weight. It made her feel unattractive and undesirable. No matter how much I assured her that I wanted her and found her sexy, she didn't feel that way herself. I've never been attracted to skinny women, preferring the curvy 'Rubenesque' look, but she just didn't feel sexy. I wished she could see herself as I did, but her self image wouldn't allow it.

When the first week of October 1999 finally arrived, we were on the dock in Sarasota awaiting the arrival of Far Horizon, our home for the week. The boat was an hour late docking, but when it finally arrived we were happy to be aboard. Captain Dave from the charter company ran us through the boats systems, then it was time for a check out cruise. I was a little intimidated by the size of the boat, which weighed 49,000 pounds. It felt like I was standing on a roof trying to drive a house. Dave had been working since 6:30 that morning, and wasn't eager to spend any more time than necessary testing my skills. When he left and pronounced us ready to cruise, I still wasn't sure I was comfortable with docking this behemoth.

Jenny and I got our bags from the car and moved aboard, starting the evening with a glass of wine on the upper deck. Then it was a dinner of fresh grouper at the dockside restaurant, and back to our boat to turn in for the evening. I just knew the week would be perfect.

The next morning we drank coffee and ate a lazy breakfast, ending with Jenny smoking and reading on the upper deck. We were both avid readers, with a favorite being John D. McDonald's Travis McGee series. We'd brought along a stack of those books, whose main character lives on a houseboat in Fort Lauderdale. We'd always found them inspiring for the waterborne lifestyle he led. McDonald had lived in Sarasota prior to his death, and we were eager to find his house on the bay.

I was ready to take the boat out, but Jenny was nervous. But of course, she was always nervous. While I was usually pretty calm dealing with stressful situations, Jenny seemed to fly apart when things got difficult. She'd once put an unfortunate end to our first trip to New York together with a panic attack as we left the city. She'd grown up in nearby New Jersey before moving South, and her view of "the city" was that you did NOT drive a car there. Her father had commuted in by train, and their visits to Manhattan were always by train and taxi. She wasn't even very comfortable with taking the subway, which I thought was the best way to get around.

David Crosby

We'd driven to New York from South Carolina, and parked the car until we left, relying on taxis and the subway. Now it was time to go home, and it was a Friday, with heavy traffic. She fretted with every block we drove, as if land mines would blow us into the sky at any moment. I just kept saying "No problem", which I thought should be comforting, but which seemed only to drive her to the verge of a nervous breakdown. The constant one way streets and no turn signs got me turned around, and her increasing panic over what was a completely non threatening situation was starting to grate on my nerves.

Then I made a wrong turn, and ended up on a bridge out of Manhattan to Newark, New Jersey, and she had a complete meltdown.

"Oh my God, we're going to Newark! Do you know how dangerous that is? I told you something like this would happen! Why didn't you bring a map? We're liable to get car jacked here. Oh God, this is a disaster!"

We ended up in a screaming match, and it just seemed like a terrible end to what had been a very nice week in New York. We'd done all the touristy things, climbed the statue of Liberty, walked in Times Square, even celebrated the Mets 1986 World Series win with a couple of million New Yorkers in a ticker tape parade, and this was how we ended the week. With a screaming fight brought on by her nerves. Now, here we were 13 years later, and she was nervous again. Not an unusual situation, but one I'd learned to be wary of. Trying to diffuse the situation by being lighthearted would only make it worse. All I could do was endure it in silence as she fretted.

Jenny reluctantly agreed to go a short way out into the bay for a picnic and swim. We got everything ready, and she cast off the lines as we pulled slowly out of the slip. The boat had been backed in, so leaving was pretty simple, and we pulled slowly through the marina past the restaurant on its pilings and the few other moored boats before we turned into the channel. I had a chart of the area, and had envisioned cruising up and down the coast during our weeks stay, but first I had to show Jenny that there was nothing to fear. We went a short way to a small barrier island on the bay that contained a park, and anchored the boat off the beach uneventfully. She relaxed a little, enjoying lunch, swimming and a beer before we decided to head back to the dock late in the day. It was a nice afternoon, and I thought things had gone well, now we just had to get back and dock it.

Jenny's anxiety increased as we approached the channel into the marina. It was a little tricky, heading towards a dead end, approaching the restaurant head on and looking down into it's windows before sliding into the channel beside it, driving straight towards a seawall and stopping a dozen feet from it to use the twin engines to pivot the boat backwards into the slip and tie up. The whole time Jenny was going "Oh my God, oh my God, Oh my God." Her anxiety was contagious, and I found myself struggling to get the boat positioned right, making three approaches before we finally made it into the slip.

We tied up, she lit a cigarette, and said "David, this boat is just too big."

"We got it docked", I replied, "What's the problem?"

"It just makes me too nervous", she answered, "I don't think I can do this." I wasn't sure why, since all she was doing was tying up the boat after docking, but her anxiety level was definitely wearing on me. After more discussion, I agreed to call Chitwood the next day and see if they could move us to a smaller boat. Jenny and I had another wonderful dinner at the marina, came back to the boat and drank wine, and crawled into the queen size bed. She always knew how to get me to go along with her wishes.

We stayed in the marina without going out that day, and did a little exploring of Sarasota by car. I felt ridiculous, being stuck at the dock, but it was the actual day of our 25th anniversary, and I didn't want to literally "rock the boat". I've never been a dock side person, always wanting to get our boats moving as soon as we got aboard. At Portman Marina on Lake Hartwell where we had kept our houseboats, there was a large group of boat owners who never went anywhere. They'd arrive Friday night, drink and party aboard all weekend, and leave Sunday night without ever having cranked the engines. Some boats hadn't left their slips in years. We called them "dock potatoes", and I certainly didn't want to become one now. I love privacy and dislike crowds, and part of the romance I imagined for this trip included exploring isolated bays, drinking wine, skinny dipping and sunbathing naked on the upper deck.

That would be tough in the marina with the Hyatt hotel's tower overlooking our slip!

I was determined not to be dock bound.

Jenny was nervous about it too, so the following day when we found a dock local who offered us a free lesson, we jumped on it. His name was Dan, and he gave us the impression that he was somehow connected to the charter company. He seemed familiar with the boat, and told us he'd been running this kind of twin diesel for over twenty years. I was a little concerned when Dan backed the boat out and spun it towards the long glass windows of the Hyatt Marina's restaurant in the opposite direction from the exit channel, but after a few tense moments, we turned back around and headed out into Sarasota Bay. Dan seemed to really know the waters, and started by taking us out New Pass into the Gulf of Mexico.

It was a tricky channel, with moving marker buoys showing the way. We surfed out through it without running aground, and then started out into the waves of the Gulf, running parallel to the shore. We were soon joined by nearly a dozen bottlenose dolphins, who started racing the bow of our little ship, leaping out of the water beneath the bow rail. Jenny and I were enthralled with the sight, and stood at the bow rail watching and taking pictures while Dan drove the boat. The dolphins left us after a few minutes, and we headed down the coast to Big Pass, where we made a long loop past the shallow water back into Sarasota Bay.

Dan then directed us across a shallow, nervously watching

the depth finder as we got near the bottom, then just making it into deeper water as we took the channel around Bird Key. The key is home to a large number of millionaires, and Dan treated us to a running commentary on the homes along the sea wall. Turned out he installed ceramic tile for a living, and has worked in many of the mansions. And we thought he worked around boats for a living! Dan & Jenny were turned around looking at a waterfall swimming pool, and I was following the channel markers when we felt a bump, and the boat lurched to a stop. We quickly saw that the channel had turned left while I went straight, and we were aground in the bend on a falling tide.

Dan took the controls and tried to back us off the sandbar, but we were grounded on the front and the side, and thoroughly stuck on an outgoing tide. We tried every trick we could think of, but finally had to give up and call Tow Boat US for help. Their Sarasota based boat was out of the water for repairs, and they had to send one from an hour away, so there was nothing to do but watch the tide fall and the sunset. It was a small runabout that showed up from TowBoat US, and after many tries and a large bill, we were still stuck.

The towboat ran Dan back to Marina Jack's, where he claimed he could round up "a dozen big boats if I need them, and we'll get you off this sandbar!" Of course that was the last we saw of him, and as darkness fell and a storm approached, we called Chitwood Charters for help. The towboat brought Captain Dave out to us, and after being stuck for four and a half hours, the tide had risen enough that he was able to back it off the sand. Captain Dave drove us back to the dock through the rain and wind, and we said an embarrassed good night.

    The next day Jenny didn't want to leave the slip, and I wasn't willing to risk ruining the week with any more excitement, so we stayed at the dock and relaxed in private with a seafood and wine dinner aboard. It rained for the third day in a row, and I was depressed about my lack of success with piloting the boat. I was known around our home lake in South Carolina as an experienced captain, having made countless trips up and down the 90 miles of Lake Hartwell in a 52 foot houseboat without serious mishap, and yet I was intimidated by the boat of our dreams. Our studio staff had given Jenny and I embroidered "Captain Crosby" and "First Mate" tee shirts as an anniversary gift, and I was too embarrassed by my performance to wear mine. I didn't feel deserving of the title "Captain".

Chapter Two

The following day I called Captain Chitwood and asked if we could "possibly move to a smaller boat?" Something we could drive a little easier.

He said he'd try, but later called back with the news that "all the boats are either out on charter or in the middle of repair projects. I'd love to help you out if I could, but I just don't have an available boat." He then offered to send Captain Dave out cruising with us. "He'd stay in the front cabin at night, and you'd never even know he was there. You'd have all the privacy you want."

Somehow I couldn't see that as our anniversary cruise, so we declined the offer, but that wasn't Captain Chitwood's only suggestion.

"We could have Captain Dave give you a lesson tomorrow, maybe get you more comfortable with the boat. How about that?"

We said yes, and made the appointment for the next afternoon. Captain Dave was out of town, so Chitwood's lead captain, Captain Rick, showed up instead.

We'd met Rick Hanson on the docks in passing and thought he seemed nice. Now he seemed very confident as he showed us how to use the dual props without touching the steering wheel to move the boat out of the slip. As we moved into the channel outside the Hyatt marina, Captain Rick pointed to the right. "That's New Pass out there past that bridge. It leads to the Gulf, but big boats like this can't use it."

"Yes they can", I answered.

"No, they can't", he came back at me, "It's too shallow."

"Oh yes they can!" was all I could say.

"Don't tell me you took this boat out New Pass?!" he asked.

Jenny and I both nodded our heads yes.

"You didn't go through the middle of the nun buoys?"

Yes again.

"Don't tell me any more', he said, "I don't want to know!"

We went farther out into Sarasota Bay, through the Ringling Causeway bridge and around the point of Bird Key as the captain continued. "To the right is Bird Key. There's a channel along the sea wall where you can get a nice view of the homes, but the only way you can get to it is go down the side channel towards the Bird Key Yacht Club and then double back around.

We pointed towards a marker and said "No it's not, you can cut right across there."

"No you can't", he replied, that's a sandbar in the middle."

"Oh yes you can!", Jenny and I both said in unison.

"Don't tell me, I don't want to know!" was all Captain Rick could say. As our cruise went on Rick would continue to point out trouble spots of shallow water with the caution that "Most people can't go through there, but maybe you folks can!" Seems our first would be instructor Dan pretended to know a lot more than he did. Rick just wanted to keep us afloat, not aground.

After having gotten off to such a bumpy start, we were finally having fun on our anniversary cruise. Captain Rick spent four hours showing us the local waters, the bird rookeries covered with snowy Egrets, miles of waterfront homes and a parade of boats traveling up and down the ICW in Sarasota Bay. We also learned a lot about Rick, as the three of us shared abbreviated life stories on the slow cruise through the numerous "No Wake, Manatee Zone" areas. We never saw a manatee, but we spent a lot of time slowing down to avoid the possibility of hitting one with our boat.

Rick sounded like he'd had a fascinating life as the stories unfolded. He was the fourth husband of his fourth wife, Dellor. He'd been a Navy demolition diver while stationed on submarines, spent six years captaining a 103 foot yacht around the world, and lived on a sailboat while cruising the Caribbean. It was when he got to the two years he'd spent in a Cuban prison that we quit trying to match stories of interesting things we'd done. Few people had lived as interesting a life as Rick Hanson, and I didn't know then that the wild stories we'd heard on our short cruise were just the beginning.

As it neared sunset, the three of us headed the boat back to the Hyatt Marina for the part I was both anticipating and dreading at the same time. Docking a 49,000 pound boat is never easy for the inexperienced captain, and the Hyatt marina is a challenge for anyone. It's a single narrow channel, faced on three sides with tall buildings so that the wind slides through it like a wind tunnel. The Chitwood Charter slips were all the way at the end, facing the long glass windows of the Boathouse, the marina restaurant. The Boathouse sits two stories high on pilings, but from the flying bridge of our boat we looked down into the dining room full of dinner guests as we made our approach.

Everyone stopped eating to watch our approach, and one diner actually got up and moved around the corner of the restaurant to get a better view of the docking. Having an audience wasn't making it any easier. With Captain Rick talking me through it, I took the boat past the restaurant all the way to the seawall, stopping just a few feet short, and then used the twin engines to walk the boat backwards into the slip. I was nervous as the stern inched it's way towards the narrow gap between the pilings, with just a foot to spare on each side, but almost before I knew it, we'd made it without so much as a bump, and were tying up the dock lines.

Captain Rick threw up his arms in a shrug and said "You can drive this boat". No problem. I was feeling pretty confident at that point, and when he mentioned as we hooked power to the boat that he would be bringing Chitwood's newest Grand Banks back from Maryland in a few weeks, my hand shot up to volunteer.

"I'd love to go if you'd like to have a free crew member." The words were out of my mouth before I had time to even think about it.

Rick surprised me by saying he'd mention it to company owner Jerry Chitwood and see what he thought. I hadn't exactly demonstrated great nautical ability over the last few days, and here I was asking him to count on me for a 1,300 mile trip. "Do you have much experience navigating on the Intracoastal?" Rick asked.

I hesitated, afraid that the truth would spoil my chances to make the trip. "No", was all I could answer.

"Well good," Rick said. "You'll get lots of practice!"

We said good night to Captain Rick, and Jenny and I poured a glass of wine and sat on the roof to celebrate the successful day.

I could hardly contain my excitement. "Do you really think they'd let me go on the trip?", I asked.

Jenny was encouraging. "I think Rick likes you, and you did great today. Maybe it will work out so you can go."

I was pleased that she was supportive of the idea. Jenny could be difficult when she didn't get her way, and I was glad not to have a battle over the possibility of being away that long.

The next day we ventured out into the bay, exploring the waterfront before anchoring for the night off Lido Beach. We relaxed off the island the next day until late afternoon and then headed for the marina. We didn't want to make an unassisted docking in the dark. As we entered the confines of the marina I saw that a glossy new 45 foot cabin cruiser was docked broadside on the seawall at the end, just where I needed to put the bow before backing into our slip.

I warned Jenny to stay calm. "Jenny, I'm going to have to drive straight towards the middle of that boat and get really close to make it into the slip. Don't panic, I won't hit it." I didn't want her to know how nervous I was about it. We were both biting our lips as I pulled the bow pulpit of the Grand Banks to within five feet of the side of the cruiser. A gust of wind or a wrong move on the throttles and it would spear that acre of fiberglass like a harpoon.

We were halfway through backing into the slip when a well dressed man walked from the restaurant to the dock just in front of us and called out "Would you like a hand?" "No thanks, we've got it under control." I added, "But we're open to suggestion!" Jenny giggled at that. I nodded towards the big cruiser we'd just come so close to and asked "Your boat?"

I wasn't surprised when "Yep" was the reply. I'm sure it got his attention watching our bow approach his boat as he ate dinner. I backed it into the slip like I'd done it a hundred times, and he helped us tie the lines. I didn't have the heart to tell him that had been our first unassisted, perfect docking! He went back to his dinner, and Jenny and I congratulated ourselves on finally conquering our fear of docking this behemoth.

After a few more days we packed and headed for home. We saw Captain Rick on the dock as we were leaving, exchanged phone numbers, and he said he'd let me know when the Maryland trip got scheduled, and he warned that it could be short notice. I was happy that he still seemed willing to take me along, but worried that if the call did come it would be at a time when I couldn't go. Most of my photography clients schedule shoots a week or two ahead of time, and I couldn't cancel on them for a personal trip.

Rick said the trip would take "a week or so", and I knew I'd do anything I could to free up the time if I got the chance. Jenny and I headed back to South Carolina, back to the daily grind, hopeful that the call would come. When a month had gone by, I figured the time was past.

Six weeks after our return, I was surprised when on a Thursday morning I answered the office phone.

"Hi David, this is Captain Chitwood, are you still interested in that trip? "

"I sure am!" I quickly replied.

"OK", he added, "Captain Rick will be leaving Maryland on Monday, can you fly up and meet him then?" My face fell.

"I have a shoot in Fort Lauderdale on Monday and Tuesday, in Charlotte on Thursday, and back in Greenville late on Friday", I answered. "Any chance you could postpone it a week?"

Chitwood wasn't encouraging. "We have to get the boat down here as soon as possible for a charter. Captain Rick wanted me to call you first, but we'll probably have to find someone else."

Damn! I really wanted to make the trip The call came, and I couldn't go. I told Chitwood that I'd double check with my clients and make sure there weren't any changes, but he didn't sound encouraging. I couldn't believe this once in a lifetime chance was going to slip away. As soon as we hung up, I called my Thursday-Friday client to make sure it was still on. They'd rescheduled this project once, maybe they'd do it again.

Nope, the client said those dates were "engraved in stone". I worked through a disappointed day until late afternoon, when I got a phone message. The "engraved in stone" dates had been postponed again! The client was apologetic, but I was thrilled.

I called Captain Chitwood right away and told him I could leave Fort Lauderdale Tuesday afternoon and fly straight to Maryland.

He said that was perfect, that the paperwork had been delayed on the boat, and Rick was leaving Maryland sometime between Wednesday and Friday, as soon as the owner could make the closing. I was on cloud nine as I finished the work week, and I packed winter clothes for the business trip to sunny Fort Lauderdale, not knowing whether I'd be home before leaving for Maryland.

Our sailing date ended up being "dawn on Friday" and I flew into Baltimore Washington Airport Thursday afternoon to meet Captain Rick.

Now we were in Oxford, Maryland, picking up the boat, and my adventure was just beginning. I was on the docks looking at the rows of Grand Banks yachts and ready to move on board. I went back into the broker's office, and the transaction hadn't made much progress. The paperwork wasn't typed up, there didn't seem to be a notary public in town available after 5 p.m., and I could tell Captain Rick was running out of patience. The broker finally got us rooms in the bed and breakfast across the street, with the promise that he'd have everything ready to sign in the morning so we could begin our journey south.

Chapter Three

Friday, November 12th

I woke to a foggy dawn on Friday, showered and threw on my clothes. I didn't see Rick in the dining room of the B&B, and ran across the street to the docks to make sure they hadn't gone to get the boat from the yard, an hour and a half cruise by water. I didn't want to miss a single part of this trip. I walked down the pretty streets of the town in the fog, and thought about what I'd learned about it from brochures the night before.

Oxford was founded in 1683, and in 1684 it and a new town called Anne Arundel (now Annapolis) were selected the only ports of entry for the entire Maryland province. It was an international shipping center until the American Revolution, which marked the end of Oxford's glory years. It enjoyed a resurgence in 1871 when the railroad arrived and improved methods of canning and packing opened national markets for oysters from the Chesapeake's plentiful oyster beds, but early in this century the oyster beds played out, and Oxford again became a sleepy little town inhabited by the watermen who still work the waters of the Tred Avon River.

Now I was looking at the Tred Avon River, but our boat still wasn't on it. I returned to the Oxford Inn, where I found Rick chatting with fellow boaters in front of the glowing fireplace in the breakfast room. He told me the closing was now set for 11am, and he wanted to be underway by noon. We left for the Trapp boat yard by car at 9:30, where Captain Rick and I finally boarded the "Waxing Gibbous". It was my first look at a 42' Motoryacht, and it was gorgeous, with the teak walls and parquet floors that Grand Banks yachts are known for.

The owner, Gene, showed us around the boat as we loaded our gear on board, with Rick taking the large master aft cabin in the stern. I threw my bags in the bow bunk room, and used the front cabin with its Vee berth as a closet and dressing room. Each end of the boat had a full head with shower, with the accommodations separated in the middle by the main salon. The "living room" or salon of the boat has an L shaped setee with folding table, a counter holding two battery operated cold plate refrigerators, and the galley with stove, sink and microwave. After we got settled, Rick checked out all the systems in the engine compartment, went to the lower helm station in the cabin and cranked the twin diesels. We backed from the slip and headed out into the placid waters of the river. Our trip south had finally begun.

Gene drove the boat from the flybridge as we passed beautiful waterfront farms at a stately eight and a half knots. Grand Banks trawlers are displacement boats, built for a smooth ride and long range, not for speed. Gene was grateful for the chance to take one last ride on his boat. He'd only had it for three years, living on it for the first two. But work had kept him away for a year, and the maintenance was getting away from him. Now he knew he needed to sell it to someone with the time to keep it up, but it was a dream he was letting go of. I asked him about the boats unusual name, and he explained.

"'Waxing' is the term used when the Moon's illuminated part is growing in size, while 'waning' means that the lighted part is decreasing. "Gibbous" means more than half, but not full. So a waxing gibbous moon is one where the reflected light is growing." I still wasn't sure that explained his reason for choosing it, but he didn't elaborate beyond that.

After a short 10 mile cruise, we docked at 11 a.m. in Oxford, but the paperwork still wasn't ready. After lunch and some grocery shopping, I hitched a ride back to the boatyard to retrieve Gene's car, which he'd agreed to let me borrow for a provisioning trip to a nearby town. There wasn't much in the way of shopping in Oxford, and we needed portable heaters, as the built in heaters on the boat weren't working.

I found a WalMart, and bought heaters, watch caps, gloves and mufflers, along with a dozen heavy athletic socks. They were items we were to be grateful for in the next few days on the chilly Chesapeake Bay. I got back to the boat at 3 p.m., and they had finished the closing. Rick was anxious to leave the dock, and so was I.

We'd talked enough in the last couple of days to start worrying that the 10 day schedule for our trip was optimistic, and it was now only 13 days until Thanksgiving.

We left the dock in Oxford at 3:30 that afternoon, ready to get the first of our 1,300 miles behind us. I took the wheel and headed into the Choptank River, enjoying the view as we passed anchored boats and modest waterfront homes along the banks. The trip down river was slow, with many no-wake zones, but when the Gibbous finally entered into the expanse of the Chesapeake Bay , we were able to get up to our cruising speed. We drove from the flybridge, which is essentially the roof of the boat with a bulkhead and windshield built in the front, and even with coats, ski masks and gloves, the November wind chill was cutting right through us as we watched the sun set.

Navigating in the frigid darkness that first night was almost more adventure than we were ready for. We had seen a couple of large ships on the bay, and the lights on our depth finder didn't work, so we were navigating off the charts by flashlight and picking out the channel markers with a spotlight. Finally at 7 p.m. we'd had enough. Captain Rick put out a call on the radio for local knowledge, and the TowBoat US office out of Solomon's talked us into a nice little place, Elizabeth Harbor Marina. They stayed with us on the radio as we picked our way up the small creek to the marina, with the only nervous moment being when the path we'd been directed on ended in a seawall in 4.9 feet of water, but we skirted the piers and found our spot.

No one was there to check us in, so we made the lines fast, hooked up the power, and made our way to the dockside Harbor Tunes restaurant for lobster and drinks. What a great finish for the day! We were exhausted after dinner, and Cap headed for his cabin while I crawled into the warmth of my sleeping bag in the front berth. We'd made less than 30 miles that afternoon, but the trip was finally underway. Counting the 10 miles from the Trappe Landing yard, we'd gone just 40 miles all together. We still had most of 1,300 miles left to go.

Chapter Four

Saturday, November 13th

We'd planned to be up at 6 a.m. for an early start, but I slept through my alarm and finally dragged myself from the warmth of the sleeping bag and out into the chilly cabin at 6:30. As soon as I got up, Rick must have heard me and stirred, and within 10 minutes the twin Lehman diesels were warming up, setting up a rumbling vibration through the hull as the boat came to life. We were still exhausted from the previous day's frigid night run, but we had a lot of miles to cover. We were heading across the Chesapeake Bay, and hoping to make Norfolk, Virginia before dark.

We'd had no time for any housekeeping or maintenance chores before leaving Oxford, and I started the morning by duct taping the sink in the tiny bow head so that I could brush my teeth. The porcelain bowls in both heads, (bathrooms for the nautically challenged), had cracked into three sections from the boat pounding the waves under its previous owner, and they had to be duct taped to be usable for the trip. The boat was scheduled for a refit in Sarasota where they would be replaced, but a temporary fix was the best we could do while underway.

I got dressed and bundled up, and we were on our way again. I made tea in the microwave for Rick and I, and we sat on the flybridge and watched the sunrise as he drove the boat back out the narrow creek we'd managed in the dark the night before.

Back in the Chesapeake, we again fought the cold and the wind as the Gibbous made it's way slowly towards Florida. We spotted a lighthouse out in the middle of the water, and the charts said it was appropriately named "Point No Point Light", a 52 foot tall stone structure that was very different from the land based light houses I was accustomed to in the Carolinas and Florida. The lighthouses I knew of were tall and narrow, while these were squatty and wide, not built to be visible from a great distance.

At 8:50 a.m. we passed the mouth of the Potomac River, and ended up behind a tug pushing a barge. Rick called him on the VHF radio and found out he was heading for Norfolk as well, so we pulled in behind him and followed his wake for the next seven hours. He was slightly faster than the Gibbous, but not by much, and following him was a lot easier than following a compass course.

Mid morning we passed Smith Point Light, another squat but pretty light house. The structure was surrounded by fishing boats, and we watched as a 20 pound striper or blue gill was hauled aboard one of them. We guessed at the weight, and later heard the fisherman say he'd caught a 20 pounder over the VHF. He didn't say 20 pound what! It was a beautiful sunny but cold day, and there were fishing boats out by the hundreds. Several times we had to change course to skirt the pack.

All through day one, and the beginning and end of day two, we were also constantly dodging through minefields of crab pot buoys, sometimes miles of them. In the open Chesapeake the water is too deep for crabbing, but everywhere else they were a constant. Under the circumstances, I thought it appropriate to have crab legs for dinner. At 11 a.m., we heard the Coast Guard out of Hampton Roads relaying an SOS. Someone had fallen overboard from the boat Kimberly Lynn, and was missing. We heard a lot of traffic about it, but didn't hear the outcome.

Before noon we passed Wolf Trap Light. The rest of the cruise was uneventful, but relaxing. We ate instant soup, then Rick found some MRE's on board. They are the military replacement for the K Rations my father experienced during World War II. Short for Meals Ready to Eat, they're supposed to be a lot tastier than the old versions. After a lesson from the Captain on the technology involved, we ate tuna casserole heated with a chemical pack. It was actually not bad, considering we had no idea how old they were.

Except for a 30 minute power nap around 1:30, I steered the Gibbous most of the day. Rick couldn't believe I wanted to drive the boat so long, and kept volunteering to take over and give me a break, but I was enjoying it. We also spent the first full day aboard getting to know each other, and sharing our life stories.

I was born a romantic. From the time I was small, I loved girls. I had my first girlfriend, Bonnie Fern, at age two, and we would hold hands and play together in the yard. The other boys thought girls were "yucky", but I loved to hang out with them. I was in love with my third grade teacher Miss Seckinger at Sexton Woods Elementary School, staying after class whenever possible. I was heartbroken when she got married over the summer. When I had my tonsils out at age four, my parents tried to make it less scary by telling me I could have all the ice cream I wanted in the hospital. All I was interested in was the pretty nurse taking care of me.

My life has always had interesting twists, and the first one came when at age five I was playing in the front yard while my mom was inside making a birthday cake for my dad's celebration that night. I ran across the street, got hit by a speeding car and dragged 60 feet. It knocked me out, and when I woke up I was underneath the car, surrounded by a view of feet.

The neighbors were all trying to decide if I was dead or not, and when I got tired of being under the car and crawled out the cries of "He's alive!" were enthusiastic. After an ambulance ride to the hospital my broken leg was put in a large cast, my abrasions were bandaged and I spent several months riding in a wheel chair and getting lots of attention. It was an auspicious start to my life of adventure.

I grew up watching movie love stories, reading King Arthur,

Peter Pan, and watching numerous musicals that my father played soundtracks from on our little hi fi. 'South Pacific' was a favorite, and the guy always sweeps the girl into his arms at the end to the tune of "Some Enchanted Evening". I just knew my life would be that way. My school days from elementary to High school were spent waiting for my true love to come onto the scene, and when I met my first serious girl friend Robin in the 11th grade, I thought she was it. We had lots of fun times double dating with friends in my VW bus, and I even took the 17 members of her high school volleyball team home in my bus one day after practice.

Alas, she was a high school girl who was less in love than I was, and when she went away to college three years later it was over.

I was in my first year of college and still looking for my true love. I'd switched cars and bought a 1969 Austin Healey Sprite, and was enjoying the top down drives back and forth between my Atlanta apartment and my parents home in Coral Springs, Florida, but none of my dates seemed to become anything but a social evening. I was always different, a quality I couldn't easily explain to the girls I dated. I was affectionate and open, not interested in the dating games that I'd seen all through high school. Other guys my age took their dates to "The Mad Hatter" at Underground Atlanta, a noisy nightclub with rock bands pounding. I wanted to sit in a quiet booth and talk to my dates, so I took them to places like "Dante's Down the Hatch", also downtown but with a substantially older crowd. I think I was a lot more comfortable with intimate conversation than my dates were.

A year later I was still looking when I first met Jenny Weller in 1973.

Jenny had lived in the same neighborhood as my family had in Florida, but I'd stayed behind in Atlanta to finish high school, and had barely met her when visiting my folks. She'd been part of my sister Karen's social circle, but they weren't what you'd call friends, more like rivals. Then Jenny had moved to Atlanta to attend Bauder Fashion College and study interior design. My sister had crashed at Jenny's campus apartment when she came to visit her Atlanta friends, and I renewed my acquaintance with Jenny. It wasn't exactly love at first sight, more like two siblings picking on each other, but I was attracted to her. We mostly teased each other, but with a tickle fight at her apartment one evening it was beginning to have physical overtones. We'd sort of had our first date when I took her to see Joni Mitchell at the Omni arena. I hadn't really planned to take her, but she was hanging out with me the day I bought the tickets, and asking her to join me seemed the thing to do.

By this time I was in my first semester at the University of Georgia in Athens 60 miles away, and was having an increasingly hard time getting free to visit Jenny. Life in Athens was exciting, and for the first time in college I was making good grades. I was also coming out of my shell of shyness. That spring of 1974, the streaking craze swept across college campuses, with naked people racing across football fields during games, and even showing up onstage at the Oscars telecast. Not wanting to be left out, student organizers at UGA decided we should set the record for the country. On March 7th, 1974, 1,543 simultaneous streakers ran across the historic old part of the 1785 era UGA campus from the arch, down Sanford Drive past the football stadium to the quad between the dorms on Lumpkin Street. There was a raucous party in the quad, and I was in the middle. I'd had the usual nightmares of being in class and realizing I was naked, but this was different. Everyone was naked, and that made it normal. And the record still stands.

I'd also found a job to augment my funds for driving to Atlanta. I worked as a security guard on a split shift with my dorm roommate Ted, with one of us working 8 to midnight, and the other working midnight to 8 a.m., switching shifts the next day. It was strange, putting on our military style uniforms and carrying an old sawed off Sears shotgun that had been assigned to us as we guarded deserted construction sites. We never loaded the two shells we were given, just carried the gun for effect. One night when Ted returned home to the dorm in uniform with the gun in hand, people on the hall panicked, and you could hear toilets flushing up and down the hall as everyone flushed their pot. It was the 70's, after all.

Ted's girlfriend Barb had been spending a lot of time with him, and I got really tired of being kept out of my dorm room for their privacy, so with the extra income from our security gig, we rented a small house trailer off campus. It was a tiny two bedroom, and it took awhile to get used to the paper thin walls. My bedroom was next to the bathroom, and one day Barb was in the shower while Ted was away. I was laying on my bed reading, and heard her drop the soap in the shower. I said in a conversational tone "You dropped the soap Barb" and she screamed.

Then it was "Oh my GOD, where are you!" She was chagrinned when she heard I was in my own room. The walls were so thin, she thought I'd walked in on her in the bathroom. Life in a trailer.

When I could get away from classes, I would drive to Atlanta to hang out with Jenny and her roommates at Bauder. We flirted, but we still had not become a couple. One night she prevailed on me to take her and Helen, one of her roommates, bowling in Atlanta. There was lots of teasing over the bowling, and I was paying, since neither Helen nor Jenny had any money. I proposed that if I won the evenings games, she'd visit me in Athens to pay me back. Helen kept egging her on, and when I finished with the high score, we both told Jenny she had to keep her bet. We picked a Friday night a week away, and I told her I'd be expecting her.

The week went by fast between work and classes, and although we'd talked a couple of times by phone, I still doubted she would actually show up. We'd planned on a cookout with Ted and Barb, and we were outdoors grilling hamburgers when Jenny drove up. I was pleased and surprised that she'd shown up, and I think she was surprised herself. There had apparently been LOTS of discussion with her roommates in Atlanta about whether she should come to Athens, the ayes winning out. And now here she was, almost as nervous about what the evening might bring as I was.

We ate dinner, drank beer and talked with my friends, and when they headed off to their bedroom late that evening, Jenny's nervousness increased. I told her I'd sleep on the couch if she'd feel better about it, but she said no, she didn't want to take my bed, we could share it. She went off to the bathroom to get ready for bed, and I crawled between the sheets to wait for her. She came back to the bedroom in a little pink teddy that she later told me her roommates had picked out for her to wear, and slid beneath the sheets.

We kissed for the first time and then much to my surprise it quickly moved to enthusiastic love making. It was wonderful to feel that she wanted to as much as I did, and afterwards we lay in bed and talked half the night. We shared hopes and dreams, and she seemed to enjoy the sharing as much as I did. That was the beginning of a three day weekend that dragged on into Monday before she finally returned to Atlanta. We spent half the weekend in bed, and the other half talking and laughing together. It was a wonderful experience, and I wondered if this was what it was like to be in love.

I called Jenny a couple of days after she left, and was puzzled by her response.

"I had a really great time this weekend", I told her.

"Me too." she replied.

Then I added "When do you think you could come up again? How about this weekend?"

"Oh", she said, "did you want to see me again?"

I was startled, and said "Hellooooo, aren't you the woman I just spent the last weekend with?! How could you ask if I wanted to see you again?"

She answered "My roommates told me you were probably just another college boy having fun, and that I'd probably never hear from you again." Her lack of confidence in my feelings surprised me, but she came up the next weekend and stayed for four days. We spent most of the balance of the semester in bed, and my previously dean's list level grades went straight in the toilet.

I still wasn't ready to call it Love, but I sure was loving our time together. Jenny moved into a two bedroom apartment in Atlanta with a room mate to stay over the summer, but quickly found herself in trouble when her roomies parents showed up and dragged her home to South Carolina. Seems that Jenny was the only one who got around to signing the lease, and she was stuck. I'd been staying with her for a week at the end of my second semester at the University of Georgia before intending to head to Chicago to spend the summer in with my folks.

When she was suddenly stuck with more rent than she could pay, I got a job at a nearby bookstore to help her with the rent.

Without planning it, we were living together. Not a good thing in a Baptist family in the South in 1974.

Chapter Five

We tried to keep our cohabitation a secret from our families, but my parents figured it out pretty quickly. My Dad kept the lines of communication open, but I wouldn't say he approved.

My Mom would only speak to me on the phone long enough to say "I know, that you know , that what you're doing is wrong."

I tried to explain that I wouldn't be doing it if I felt it was wrong, but she wouldn't hear it.

She just kept repeating that "I know, that you know, that what you're doing is wrong".

It put a lot of strain on me, and my brother Stephen and sister Karen, who were living at home with my folks, added to it by telling me how much angst it was causing at home. "Why don't you just come home for the summer, and then see her again in the Fall?" was their suggestion.

Nobody seemed to understand how I felt. They just wanted peace at home. I didn't feel I could abandon Jenny to her debts. By the end of the summer I was in love. Maybe it was just the shared responsibilities, having someone really need me, but I sure thought I was in love.

After several months of difficult phone calls with my family in Chicago, it all came to a head. We were planning a visit to my parent's house, and my Mom didn't want me to bring Jenny. And, unbeknownst to me, Jenny was planning on backing out of the trip at the last minute. She couldn't face the pressure of seeing my family when she felt unwelcome. During a particularly difficult phone call with my family while at an old friends house, she walked out. I went looking for her, and found her sitting on the curb of my childhood elementary school a few blocks away, crying.

She said "I'm just going to disappear, go to Alaska or something and you'll never see me again. I'm making you miserable!"

I said that not only did I not want her to run away, I wanted her to marry me.

Jenny was skeptical, thinking it was a reaction to her distress.

I told her I had been planning to ask her somewhere more romantic, on her late grandfather's Indiana farm that we had planned to visit on our trip to Chicago. Now suddenly seemed like a better idea.

And so, at barely 21 years old, I was engaged. We packed up

her apartment, begged for mercy on the lease from the landlady, put all of our possessions in a storage building, and headed for Chicago. We stopped in Winnimac, Indiana, to see her grandfather's farm, and that was a disaster. The land was leased to other farms, and no one lived in the house that held such fond memories for Jenny. We found the key and let ourselves in. Shortly after our arrival, the phone rang.

She answered it, and found it was a curious neighbor wanting to know who was visiting the house.

"I'm Ernst Baumann's granddaughter, just visiting on my way up north", she told them.

The neighbor seemed to accept the answer, and said her goodbyes. We were a little nervous about being discovered there so quickly, but we couldn't afford a motel room, and tried to settle in for the night. That evening the phone rang again.

"What are you doing in MY father's house with THAT BOY?" her mother said in her imperious voice.

Jenny stammered that we were just stopping for a quick look around on our way to Chicago, and that we weren't staying. Her Mother gave her the third degree, but she seemed to convince her that we'd be on the way soon. We'd been ratted out by the nosy neighbor.

Actually, leaving wasn't an option. We were 100 miles from any big city, with no money for a motel. So we turned out the lights, avoided the windows, and spent a miserable night hiding in the house. At dawn the next morning, we headed for Chicago, hoping for a warmer reception.

Things were pretty chilly when we arrived at my parents. They were happy to see me, but not so thrilled with my bringing Jenny. It took me a while to get up the nerve to tell them we were engaged . Since they seemed so opposed to her as my companion, I was worried about their reaction when I told them she was joining the family.

Boy was I wrong. When I told them we were getting married, all was forgiven.

Son! Daughter-in-law! Welcome to the family! It still doesn't make sense to me, but getting married would make everything right. The visit went fine after that, although my Mom made sure that we knew we would NOT be sharing a bedroom in her house until we got married.

After a week, we headed south to Fort Lauderdale to tell the news to Jenny's parents. In spite of the hot Florida weather, that reception was really chilly. They had unbeknownst to us just discovered that we were living together, and the news that we were getting married didn't seem to lessen their disapproval at all.

Her Father sprung it on me over our arrival day dinner. I'd left the table to take a call from my parents, and when I came back, Jenny and her Mother were crying.

As I sat down, her father said, "So, I understand you're living together, is that correct?"

I quietly said yes, and the crying from Jenny and her mom got louder. But that wasn't enough for him.

"I don't mean sharing the apartment," he continued. "I mean sharing the marriage bed, living together as man and wife!"

I miserably answered "Yes", and the crying got still louder.

He replied, "Well, I hope you both know we're VERY disappointed in you." Then he added, "Jenny, are you pregnant?"

She finally showed a little spirit as she angrily told him no, but they weren't through with us yet.

They started planning our wedding on the spot, and Jenny's mom, being a nurse, said "I can get the blood tests rushed. We can have the wedding in two days!"

We weren't about to have a shot gun wedding in that hostile environment, and told them we were getting married in Atlanta when we returned home.

It was a very tense and uncomfortable visit, and set the stage for many such visits with Jenny's parents over the next twenty years.

We finally escaped back to Atlanta, found an apartment, had a hastily arranged wedding at the Baptist Church I'd grown up in, and began married life in October of 1974.

We couldn't afford a honeymoon, but my parents arranged for a room at the downtown Atlanta Hyatt for the wedding night. When we showed up in our wedding clothes, the desk clerk put us in a suite at no extra cost. It seemed
like a good start to our life together, and I began looking for a job.

I'd worked at bookstores in high school and college, and that's where I went first. No luck. Then I went to all of the department stores within 10 miles. Still no luck. After three weeks looking without success and the rent coming due, I was starting to get desperate. I went 15 miles out, and was interviewing at J.C. Penney for a sales job. The answer wasn't what I expected.

The HR person said "We don't have anything in the store, but there is an opening on the gas island."

I wasn't thrilled, but I took it. So for the next eight months, I drove 14 miles in Atlanta traffic to my job pumping gas for $2. an hour. About $66. a week after taxes. Home was a two bedroom apartment for $136.50 a month. There went half of my salary. With a $52. car payment, a $21. payment on a stereo, insurance and utilities, there was nothing left to buy food with. My parents sent us $100. a month, and that was our food budget. Even in 1974 dollars, it was hard to make ends meet. We were poor, but relatively happy.

Jenny and I had each spent time in college prior to getting married, and we both wanted to finish. We decided to each take a year at a time in school while the other one worked, and I offered to let her take the first year. She enrolled in nearby DeKalb Community College, a five minute bus ride away.

For me, it wasn't the easiest life, pumping gas eight hours a day, but it wasn't that hard either. In the days before self service, my only job was to pump gas, and I filled my time between customers with reading. If no cars were at the pumps, I had no other duties. I could get through a paperback book most days, and larger volumes never took more than three days. The hardest part was making so little money, and coming home every night smelling like gasoline. It got tougher in the winter, when I spent my days huddled in front of the heater in the little metal gas island building.

A month into our marriage, the first signs of trouble appeared. Every night when I came home and asked how school was going, Jenny told me it was "Fine", and gave a few classroom details. One night in bed, the truth came out. She began crying, and tearfully admitted that she quit school weeks ago!

She had been too ashamed to admit it, so she'd been lying every day when she answered my "How was school today?" question. I was dismayed by this, but she was so upset I did my best to comfort her.

I also told her that she should never be afraid to tell me the truth, even if it wasn't pretty. Turns out she'd felt so much pressure from her parents to finish school that she couldn't concentrate, and she just stressed out.

Things rocked along after that, with Jenny staying home learning to be a homemaker and playing with the two dogs she'd brought home from the Humane Society while I pumped gas all day. When she brought the second one home, I pitched a fit.

"We can barely feed ourselves, and you're bringing dogs home every other week! What were you thinking?" That led to my coming home the next night and finding her in complete meltdown mode. "What's wrong?" I asked.

She sobbed out the answer. "You didn't want her, so I took her back to the Humane Society."

Next thing I knew, we were down at the shelter, looking for our new dog Carly to rescue her a second time. We had to pay a second adoption fee and got lectured by the staff, but it felt like a crisis averted.

Then things got much worse.

Jenny had an auto accident, ruled her fault by the police on the scene, and did serious damage to our little Opel Manta Rallye, our only transportation. She was unhurt, but the car was not drivable and would be in the shop for weeks. Insurance would pay for the repair, but not for a rental car. I was at a loss. How would I get to work every day? My tiny income was all we had, there had to be a way. I searched the classifieds and found a beat up Kawasaki 90 motorcycle that a kid had been riding in his parents back yard. I borrowed the $100. cost from a friend and bought it over the weekend.

The bike was a disaster. It had a brake linkage held together with a paper clip, a muffler sealed with tin foil, no inspection sticker, and an expired tag that wasn't mounted on the bike. I had no cycling experience and lacked the required motorcycle driver's license, but I had no choice. Monday morning I hopped on for the fourteen mile ride to work. I tried to take back roads to avoid the interstate, which turned out to be the right idea. Half way there the muffler fell off. I retrieved it and hid it behind a tree to pick it up on the way home. After another mile, the plug fouled out on the single cylinder engine and the bike sputtered to a stop. I pushed it two miles until I reached a lawnmower repair shop, and the owner managed to find a plug which fit well enough to get me the rest of the way to work. By this time I was two hours late. I'd only been working the gas island a couple of weeks, but they were pretty understanding of my dilemma.

On my lunch hour I went to a nearby motorcycle shop and got the correct plug, practiced my riding in the parking lot, and called a neighbor to follow me home after work to pick up the muffler. So far, so good. On the trip home, nervously trying to keep the bike on the road, I got stopped for speeding. I couldn't believe it!

What else could go wrong? I sat in the back of the police car and poured out my sad story to the officer. Newly married, no money, wife wrecked the car. He was so sympathetic that he was writing me a warning! No inspection sticker, no muffler, no motorcycle driver's license, speeding and still he was writing me a warning. I was so grateful for his compassion.

He'd done a routine license check, and I was stunned when I heard a dry voice over the radio say "That tag is reported stolen."

The cop turned around and looked sadly at me and said "Well son, that changes everything. Put your hands on the seat where I can see them and don't move."

I was terrified. I assured him I had checked everything out on the bike when I bought it. Frame numbers, fork numbers, motor numbers, everything!

I just hadn't thought to check the expired tag against the title.

My neighbor had been following me home from work to pick up the muffler, and he found a pay phone and called home to tell his wife to let Jenny know what was going on. "David got stopped for speeding," he told her, "and now there's five police cars here and they're frisking him!" It must have been a slow night in DeKalb County, Georgia, because a large portion of the police force showed up to see what was going on. A plainclothes detective unit was even dispatched to question me on the scene. A very pleasant woman, Detective Hawes, sat in the back seat of the police car as I frantically gave her the details.

"Calm down, don't worry", she assured me, "It sounds like you didn't do anything wrong." Then she added "But we have to start somewhere, so you're under arrest."

I protested, but there was no stopping it. I was taken to the DeKalb County jail for mug shots and fingerprints, and they took my clothes and gave me a prison jumpsuit and flip flops so I couldn't hang myself with my shoe laces.

I was put in a large cell with 25 other inmates, and within minutes one of them walked up to where I sat disconsolately on a bunk and asked me "What are you in for?" It felt like I was living a bad movie. I couldn't believe this was happening to me.

They let Jenny see me briefly, and she said she was trying to get me out. She'd gone home to make phone calls to try and raise the bail money, and my Father had chosen that moment to call and check on the newlyweds. "Hi Jenny", he greeted her jovially.

"It's your new father-in-law. How are the newlyweds today?"

She stammered "Well..., well..., well... David's in jail!"

He'd listened as she poured out the story, and said he'd call a lawyer he knew in Atlanta, an old family friend. Back at the jail, a judge finally set bail at $1,500., and after borrowing the $150 bail bondsman's fee from another friend, I was released. It was midnight, and I had been first pulled over by the cop at 5:30 in the afternoon.

It all seemed so crazy. I called my lawyer, and he said the police seemed unwilling to drop it. After a few weeks, he discovered that the police even knew who was responsible. The motorcycle had originally belonged to a notorious motorcycle thief in Gwinnett County, another Atlanta suburb, and he had sold it to the family I bought it from. The Kawasaki was completely legal, but he had mistakenly given them a stolen tag. The bike it came from was stolen three blocks from this crooks house. They had everything but signs and arrows pointing to his guilt. But he was in another county, not their jurisdiction. Not worth going after.

And what about me? Surely now they'd drop the charge, which was a felony, theft of a motor vehicle ID.

But no. If they dropped it, there would be an open, unsolved case on the books. That messes up their crime statistics, which affects their federal funding. They needed me on the hook, so they offered a plea bargain. I was outraged! Not only had I done nothing wrong, they knew it! They just didn't care. And so it dragged on.

Another month later, near Christmas, there came a knock on my apartment door at 5 a.m. I stumbled sleepily to the door in my bathrobe, wondering what was wrong. People didn't often show up at my door at that hour. I opened it to the sight of two large DeKalb County Sheriff's deputies, dressed in their uniforms and Mountie style hats.

"Are you Alan David Crosby?" one of them asked.

When I answered yes, he said "We have a warrant for your arrest for failure to appear for your trial."

I was flabbergasted. I told them I'd never been given a trial date, even though my attorney was in constant contact with them.

"Tell it to the judge." was all they would say.

They followed me into the bedroom and watched me get dressed to prevent me from escaping out a window, and my wife, naked under the covers, told them to "Get the hell out of our bedroom!"

She was told "Watch your mouth, or we'll take you in too."

And so I was dragged out the front door before dawn, handcuffs behind my back as the neighbors all watched from their porches, lit by the blue lights flashing on the police cars. The first time I'd been arrested I was scared. Now I was just angry. I couldn't believe they could make such a stupid mistake. Boy, was I surprised. When I contacted the bondsman who bailed me out the first time, he refused to talk to me. When I contacted another one, he told me why.

"The other guy is mad because he just lost $1,500."

I said "But he'll get his money back since they screwed up, won't he?"

He explained, "Here's how it works. We're licensed by the county to work out of the jail. Every now and then they yank one of our bonds after not giving them a trial date. If we complain, we lose our right to work out of the jail, which we means we go out of business.
They make a little extra money, and we can't stop it. But it doesn't make us very happy, and that's why he wouldn't take your call."

I was shocked at the corruption, and angry that I was the victim of it.

My case dragged on unresolved for several more weeks, until a call from my attorney brought the news that it was being "dropped for lack of evidence." When I protested that the charges should have been dropped period, he explained that would leave an unsolved crime on the books. Bad for crime statistics. This way, I was on record as arrested for the crime, then released because the evidence was insufficient to take me to trial. The injustice of it appalled me. I asked my lawyer about suing them for false arrest. The answer was just as disappointing as the rest of this sorry mess.

"You'd be suing the county, in the county, under a county judge", he told me. "You'd lose, and they'd never let you live in peace in this county again".

By that time, I was ready to believe the worst. The abuse of power and indifference toward justice was something I would not have believed if it hadn't happened to me.

And this was suburban Atlanta, not some little backwater town! My faith in the legal system took a dive after that.

And so began my life with Jenny.

Chapter Six
Saturday November 13th

Captain Rick and I had talked for hours as we drove the Gibbous through the frigid Chesapeake Bay, but as the traffic increased when we neared our port for the night, it was time to concentrate on piloting. We approached Norfolk by way of the Thimble Shoals lighthouse around 4 p.m., and it made some great photos, surrounded by sailboats with a giant container ship in the background. Rick took the wheel while I took a few shots. We started seeing a lot of ship and barge traffic as we neared the harbor and passed through the Norfolk Navy yard. It was quite a scene, starting with four aircraft carriers, lined up like giant vehicles in a parking lot. We saw just about every kind of Navy ship, including five fast attack subs, dangerous looking even in their mothballed state.

Navigating our little vessel thru the giants and the tugs and barges under a red sunset was great fun, and made me feel like I was captaining my own little ship. Just after dark, we tied up at the Waterside Marina in Norfolk. It's next to a shopping area with a Hooters restaurant directly out front. It was a little too busy and noisy for me, but Rick likes a crowd.

After a dinner during which we watched my Georgia Bulldogs go down 31 - 0 to Auburn in the first half of a game on the bar TV, we went back to the boat for a little maintenance. I headed to the marina showers to clean up while Rick changed the fuel filters on the engines, which he said were as dirty as any he'd ever seen. A hot shower is a hard thing to come by on a boat, and I took my time steaming off the cold miles through the Chesapeake. Rick was still at his chores when I got back, so I hosed down the boat and the decks, took out the trash, and sat down to catch up on my travel notes. We'd traveled 100 miles that day, 140 total for the trip.

The peaceful waters had given us lots of time to talk, and Rick was curious about whether my life with Jenny had gotten any better after the rocky start. I continued my story, back at the Penney's gas pumps. It was obvious from her rapid departure from school that she wasn't ready for college yet, so we made plans for my return to school. I was farther along than she was, with two years under my belt, so it seemed to make sense to both of us for me to return to UGA, get my degree and start making a real living.

Jenny hadn't adjusted very well to our low standard of living.

We'd both grown up middle class, not pampered but well provided for, and she just wasn't used to this much struggling to survive. Typical of the kind of exchanges we had was the debacle after our first Thanksgiving together. My parents had sent money for a turkey, and we'd been eating the leftovers for a week. We'd had turkey and vegetables, turkey sandwiches, turkey soup, just about every kind of turkey dish you can imagine. Now Jenny was making turkey divan, a casserole with turkey, broccoli and cream of mushroom soup. She'd arranged the last of the turkey in the Corning Ware dish, laid out the broccoli, and had set the dish atop the old round topped refrigerator to free up space as she sliced the broccoli into strips. When she closed the refrigerator door after getting cheese out to top it all off, the lid slipped off the edge and crashed into the casserole dish and onto the floor, scattering the ingredients among the slivers of glass.

Jenny was hysterical. She just fell apart, and kept wailing "I can't live like this!"

I tried to calm her down as I looked at the last of our food supply lying in ruins on the floor.

"Hey, I told her, "This is not that bad. We're just starting out, this is the bottom of the ladder for us, from here on things will get better. And look at what we already have. A two bedroom apartment, a TV, a stereo, a car, two dogs and a cat. And this is the bottom for us. What we have now is more than a lot of the world will ever have, even in this country. And for us, it's just the beginning."

Her reply was disappointing. "I don't care, I can't live like this!" she wailed.

Less than two months into our marriage, I could see I had my work cut out for me.

I've always been something of a rescuer, and boy, did Jenny need some rescuing! She was adopted as an infant, and her parents were formal, somewhat stiff and cold people. I'd grown up in a warm hugging family, and couldn't relate to the distance she was used to in personal relationships. Her brother Todd had been adopted when she was three, and he was the family bad boy. He'd been difficult since birth, and had dropped out of school at 15.

Jenny's parents made it clear they expected more from her, and the pressure of their expectations had always made her feel like an unloved failure. I tried to reassure her that I loved her just the way she was, but she didn't exactly make it easy. She seemed to resent the easy relationship I had with my parents, even though they had done their best to make her feel a part a part of the family after our wedding. We'd just have to work on it.

After eight months of pumping gas, I was ready for a change. I thought if we moved to Athens, where the University of Georgia is located, it would be easier to have that out of the way when I started back to school, so I went job hunting there, and we began looking for a place to live. Apartments were expensive with the growing student population, and Jenny wanted something more house-like. I didn't know then that her desire for better living quarters than we could really afford was the beginning of a 25 year long struggle.

We found a barrel shaped house in Crawford, Georgia, 14 miles outside of Athens. It had two bedrooms, high ceilings and a spiral staircase, and was on a couple of acres of land. It was half of a duplex, and the long distance from Athens made the rent a bargain. We signed a one year lease and moved in. I had a few days to move before starting my new job at the Holsum Bread Company, where I'd be a route sales driver. We got everything moved, and met our neighbor Judy, who worked at the Veterinary School at Georgia. She also raised AKC Rottweilers and showed them at regional dog shows.

Judy wasn't thrilled when we first moved in, the young newlyweds with the two mutts, but she got used to the idea. Jenny was home all day while I worked, and the two of them got to be friends over time. My wife was also somewhat easily impressed, and she soon fell under the spell of "pure bred dogs." I thought one dog was as good as another, but was treated to endless lectures about various breeds and their many purposes in life. Never mind that very few of them were ever used for the purposes they were bred for, but had generally become costly pets. Jenny and Judy started going off to weekend dog shows together while I worked, and it was much later that I realized what an expensive hobby she'd picked for herself. I was just glad she'd found something to enjoy.

Meanwhile, I was off to make a living. Holsum Bread was

like most other route sales jobs, long hours of grinding work. They started me in training at $150. a week, and compared to the $66. a week I'd made pumping gas, I felt well compensated. But I still didn't know how hard I'd be working to earn it.

The first week was a disaster. My shift started at 5:30 a.m., and I needed to leave Crawford by just after 5 a.m. to make it on time. I set my alarm for 4:30, and awoke at 6, in a panic. I was at work by 7 a.m., and they were pretty understanding, as it was a common problem for new hires. I spent the first four days oversleeping and then being sent to help an experienced driver with his route, which consisted mainly of stocking Holsum Bread on the shelves of large grocery stores. Even with setting four alarm clocks, I just couldn't seem to wake up at 4:30 a.m.

When on Friday I overslept again, I rushed straight to the grocery store where I knew the driver would be at that time, hoping to skip the chewing out at the office. When I arrived, he told me the bad news. I wasn't assisting him today, I was scheduled to drive a truck loaded with bread to Toccoa, Georgia to help out another driver. I raced back to the bakery, where I was scolded by my supervisor, and sent off in the truck to Toccoa. I couldn't believe I hadn't been fired already, but I knew I was on thin ice.

The funny thing is that I never over slept again. After the first week, I popped out of bed without fail when the alarm went off at 4:30. I'd just needed the time to adjust. After the first trying

week, things went pretty well. I spent some time assisting on other routes, and then my supervisor started training me for my own.
He was experienced and speedy, and the days seemed to fly by. We'd load the truck starting at 5:30 a.m., stop for a quick breakfast at 6, and then head out on the route.

It was 25 stops spread over 200 miles, the second worst route in the bakery. Perfect for the new guy.
There were a few grocery stores, which is where the real money is made, but there were also a lot of mom and pop country stores, where you'd drop off six loaves of bread and a few packaged sweets, and hope they'd have sold at least half of it when you came back the next day. Once I took over the route solo, I'd be on straight commission. The rates were from six cents for a large loaf of bread down to one half a cent for sweets. Very unprofitable at those small country stores, but important for keeping the Holsum brand in front of the public, or at least, that's what I was told.

Even with the help of my speedy supervisor, we were working 12 hour days. We'd get back to the bakery around 4:30 p.m., and spend the last hour unloading the truck of the day old bread and out dated sweets, then running totals and turning in the days receipts. I'd be out at 5:30 and home before 6 p.m., ready for an evening with my new bride. We were moving so fast that the work days flew by, and the 60 hours a week I was working seemed a fair trade for my new salary. I had Wednesdays and Sundays off, and life seemed pretty good.

We only had one car, so Jenny was housebound, only getting

out when I was off from work or when she went out with our neighbor Judy. I didn't see it then, but this was probably the beginning of one of Jenny's frequent depressions, something that would plague us for years to come.

In that first month driving the bread truck, my birthday came around. I was turning 22 years old, and the day before Jenny told me she was upset that she couldn't go shopping for any way to celebrate the day because of her lack of transportation.

I told her not to worry, that it was no big deal, but I admit I expected she would do something. I left for the bakery long before she woke up, and when I got home, I thought I'd get a "Happy Birthday!", a home made card, maybe even a cake. A present wasn't even necessary.

Instead I got a "How was your day?" and a quiet supper. I kept thinking she had some kind of surprise in mind, but by bed time there had still been absolutely no mention of my birthday. As a kid my Mom had always made a big deal of our birthdays, and I was kind of shocked that mine was going to pass by without a word said about it by my new bride.

As we lay in bed I finally asked Jenny, "Are you not going to say anything about my birthday at all?"

"You told me not to worry about it!" she replied. Somehow I hadn't thought that meant it would vanish completely, and I told her that I just hoped for some mention of the event.

She started crying that "You know I don't have a car, I'm stuck here all day, what was I supposed to do!"

I said that a hand drawn card would have been fine, but by that point she was inconsolable.

Happy Birthday to me.

The lack of transportation became an increasing problem, and while we couldn't afford a second car, I knew I had to do something. I found a bargain price on a Yamaha 175 dirt bike, and thought that might solve our dilemma. My previous motorcycling experienced consisted of the one day I had driven the Kawasaki 90 in Atlanta before being arrested for the stolen tag. I thought I was better prepared this time. The trip was still a 14 mile ride to work, but it was on a two lane country road, and I thought I could handle it.

My parents weren't happy that I would be riding a motorcycle, but they couldn't complain too loudly, as they had ridden their Cushman scooter over 300 miles to see my grandparents when they were newlyweds in the 1940's.

We got a loan from my Grandfather, bought the bike, and I started taking it to work at 5 a.m. every morning. The chill cut right through my clothes at that time of the morning, and by the second week I bought a snowmobile suit to wear on the drive. It kept me warm when I was moving, but I would start pouring sweat anytime I had to stop at a light. At least I was mobile, and Jenny was able to drive herself to Athens to look for a job. She found one in book keeping at Davison's Department store downtown, an old gray stone monstrosity that was built long before the days of malls. She was in the offices on the mezzanine, and having work and purpose seemed to lift her depression. Things got better at home, at least for the limited time I was there.

Meanwhile, the bread truck job was killing me. I'd graduated to doing my route solo, and I was overwhelmed. What had been possible with my fast moving supervisor's help was a constant struggle for me. The 12 hour days quickly became 14 and 15 hour days, and I was pushing every day just to make it through. Then one morning I woke up and couldn't bend over to tie my shoes. My back was locked up tight, and I was in a lot of pain. We didn't have a phone, so I had Jenny drive me into the bakery, where I explained the problem to my supervisor Jimmy. He wasn't very happy, but I headed for the doctor, leaving Jimmy to run my route. The doctor told me I had sprained my back, and gave me electric shock therapy to the muscles, along with a prescription for a weeks worth of muscle relaxers.

A sprained back at 22 years old, I couldn't believe it! My friends and family had a hard time understanding how I sprained my back carrying bread, but the explanation was simple. Take a metal tray, and put 10 loaves of bread on it. Then stack them four high, and lift those 40 loaves and four metal trays up and down, up and down, up and down, for 12 plus hours a day. One day, your back says "Enough already!" And mine had definitely had enough.

I stopped by the bakery that afternoon and told Jimmy the news. He would have to drive, as I was not allowed to drive while taking the muscle relaxers. I was also not supposed to do any lifting for a week. I could ride along and do the paperwork at each stop, but that was it. He wasn't very happy, but there wasn't much choice. The first couple of days went ok, but by the end of the week Jimmy had me carrying the bread again as I recovered. My back held out, but it was the beginning of years of lower back pain. By Monday I was on my own again, and struggling to keep up. The 14 and 15 hour days were now stretching to 16 and even 17 hours as my body wore down. Some of the country stores at the end of the route closed for the day before I could get to them, and a few complained to the bakery about having to sell day old bread. I was struggling, but doing the best I could. I'd get up at 4:30 a.m., and was getting done as late as 10:30 at night, putting me home at 11 p.m. The exhaustion was making my paperwork take twice as long, as I was too exhausted to think straight. Then my supervisor added a new twist.

"Fred's Grocery" was a medium size store on my route in Madison, Georgia. It was in an old former A&P store front, and usually sold about 40 loaves a day of Holsum Bread, a small amount for a grocery. The grocery business is all about shelf space, and the Colonial Bread driver had four times the space we did. Well, Jimmy had a plan to get more of it. We'd put on a sale, two loaves for a dollar. And we'd put 500 loaves of bread in the store. I was appalled. "Jimmy, he only sells about 40 loaves a day for us at that store! This will be a big waste of time and money." He wouldn't listen, convinced that the sale would be a big success, and that Fred would reward us with a bigger slice of his limited shelf space. I argued against it to no avail, and Jimmy scheduled the sale for Monday of the next week. I spent my Sunday off dreading Monday. Delivering 500 extra loaves would be a lot of work, and whatever hadn't sold would just have to be picked up Tuesday. And I wouldn't make a penny for unsold bread.

Monday morning I arrived at the Holsum Bakery and was met by Jimmy at the door.

"David, I want you to meet Chip. He's a new trainee this week, and he's going to help you on the route today since you're doing the sale at Fred's." Help would be a relief, but it still wasn't going to make the day easy.

I showed Chip the ropes as we loaded my truck. We had several rolling racks in the aisle to accommodate the extra 500 loaves we were carrying, and by 6 a.m. we were packed to the gills.

Chip and I stopped for a quick breakfast as we left the bakery on our 200 mile route, and then headed out of town towards our first stop. This was his first day on the job, and he had all of the typical new employee questions as we drove through the Georgia countryside. It was overcast at 6:30 a.m., and rain was predicted, which would only make the day longer.

"What time do we break for lunch?" Chip asked.

I told him "We get to Madison, Georgia at noon, and our first stop is a Dairy Queen. We go in and place our lunch orders, and then deliver their buns while it's cooking. Then we sit for about 10 minutes and eat before heading to our next stop."

Chip was starting to look a little worried as he asked "What time is our break?"

I answered "There's a Mom and Pop grocery way out in the country that we hit about 3:30 this afternoon. We'll get a soft drink there, and get a sweet roll off the truck. We have a 25 mile drive to the next store, and that's our break."

Now he looked really concerned as he asked "What time will we be done for the day?"

I said "Well, with these 500 extra loaves we'll be busting our butts all day. But if we really hustle, we can make it back by 8:30." My sidekick for the day looked really confused as he said "But that's only two hours from now!"

"No," I answered, "I mean 8:30 tonight!"
Fourteen more hours of work to go. He looked stunned as I added "And the first thing Jimmy will say when we walk back in the door is "What took you so long!"

Somehow I think the next 14 hours were as enlightening for me as they were for Holsum's newest employee. We raced through every stop, flinging bread on shelves as we ran to the truck and back. Cramming the 500 extra loaves into Fred's Grocery was just as big a pain as I'd anticipated, and I knew I would likely be picking much of it up the next day, unsold and unprofitable. Chip was full of questions, and the more I told him about the work of being a "bread man", the more absurd it seemed. By the time we were rolling back through Madison, Georgia at 7:45 at night, my mind was made up. We looked through the windows of the closed

Fred's Grocery, and saw at least 400 loaves of Holsum Bread still cramming the shelves. What a nightmare for somebody. But it didn't have to be me.

We drove back to Athens, pulled into the bakery right at 8:30 p.m. as I'd predicted, and the first thing out of my supervisors mouth was "What took you so long!?"

I only had one answer for that. "I quit." That was the last thing Jimmy wanted. If I quit, he'd have to run my route until a replacement was hired and trained. AND he'd have to pick up the more than 400 loaves of day old bread at Fred's Grocery!

"Now David", he said, "Let's not be hasty. I'll unload your truck for you while you go do your paperwork and count the money."

I went into the office without a word, where I spent the next half hour running totals and sorting receipts.

Jimmy came in just as I was finishing, and said
"So, have you had time to reconsider?"

I said "Yes, and I still quit."

Now he turned to insults. "What's the matter, aren't you a man? You some kind of pussy? Can't do the work that real men do?"

I knew he was just trying to pressure me to stay, and replied "Call me whatever you want, I still quit!" I gathered my coat, hat and gloves, and left the bakery that night with his insults still echoing off the walls. I got home completely worn out, told Jenny what had happened, and slept for nearly 24 hours as the exhaustion of the job finally caught up with me.

Walking off the job was something I wasn't used to doing, but it sure felt justified in this case. I spent the next week recuperating, and then found a full time job in the Men's Department at Davison's. Jenny and I could ride in together to work, and I would move to part time as soon as school started back at UGA.

Life started to seem normal again.

Chapter Seven
Sunday, November 14th

I awoke late at 7 a.m., wondering why we hadn't left at dawn. Rick popped his head in the boat and said he'd found a grocery within walking distance, and was going to see if he could get provisions. I quickly got dressed and ready, and when Rick got back and told me it was open, I walked to the Provisioning Center, a nice little grocery a few blocks from Nauticus, the Norfolk maritime museum located near our berth at the Waterside Marina. The store was pricey but nice, and I stocked up for the next few days on things we could eat on the run.

'Provisioning' means different things depending on the boat you're on, and the store obviously was used to folks from some of the fancier yachts. There was caviar, artichoke hearts, exotic spices and fine wines. Fortunately, they also had instant soup and vienna sausages for us 'low brow' boaters. Rick and I needed food we could heat and eat quickly with nothing but a microwave, since we wouldn't be stopping the boat to prepare elaborate meals. The walk past the maritime museum, with it's tug boat museum out back, made me add this to the list of places I wanted to come back and spend more time in. When I got back to the dock, Captain Rick was chatting with the owner of Sea Dream, a nice old wooden Trumpy motoryacht tied up off our stern. Its varnished wooden cabin exterior looked like it belonged in the 1930's. Rick was ready to be underway, and we departed around 8 a.m.

The trip out of Norfolk was almost as interesting as the arrival had been, with aircraft carriers and mothballed navy ships of distant vintage giving way to rusty freighters bound for China. We had to wait for a couple of lift bridge openings, and it's an awesome sight watching the steel structure rise on giant chains above your head.

We entered the Dismal Swamp Canal opening around 8:30, and called the operator at the Deep Creek Lock.

He said he had just opened the lock, and the next opening was at 11. We got there around 9 a.m., so we anchored and caught up on naps and maintenance while we waited. Ark, an attractive green steel hulled sailboat, waited at anchor in front of us.

The Dismal Swamp Canal is the oldest man made waterway in the United States, with construction begun in 1793 to move goods by water from Virginia to North Carolina. Dug completely by hand, the 22 mile waterway opened for traffic in 1805.

At about the time the canal opened, the Dismal Swamp Hotel was built astride the state line on the west bank. It was a popular spot for lover's trysts as well as duels; the winner was rarely arrested as the dead man, as well as the crime, were in another state. As the state line split the main salon, the hotel was quite popular with gamblers who would simply move the game to the opposite side of the room with the arrival of the sheriff from the other jurisdiction. No trace of the hotel can be found today. The canal was important in the Civil War during the Battle of South Mills. Union forces learned of rumors that it would be used to help the Confederate ironclad CSS Virginia escape from Hampton Roads, and troops destroyed the Culpepper Locks near South Mills to prevent the escape.

The war left the canal in a terrible state of repair, making travel difficult. In 1892 Lake Drummond Canal and Water Company launched rehabilitation efforts, and once again a steady stream of vessels carrying lumber, shingles, farm products and passengers made the canal a bustling interstate thoroughfare. By the 1920's, other forms of transportation reduced traffic on the canal drastically, and in 1929 it was sold to the federal government for $500,000. As recreational boating became popular in the mid 20th century, the canal became an important link to provide shelter from the often treacherous weather on the Atlantic Coastline off the Carolinas and the Virginia Capes. (Wikipedia)

Now we were about to enter the historic waterway. A little before 11, the gates opened, and I took the helm, following Ark into the lock chamber. I had never been through a lock before, but had read a little about it and had an idea of what to expect. This one raised the water level about six feet, so we held lines looped around pilings at the top of the wall as the water rushed in, tightening the lines as we went up. As we rose to the top the lockmaster gave us instructions, cautioned us against speeding to the next lock, saying there was a six knot limit. The canal had just reopened two weeks before, three hurricanes having ravaged the area in the last year, and the control depth was only five feet. Gibbous draws about four and a half feet, not a lot of margin for error. Capt. Rick asked him about running at night, saying we had to at least make Elizabeth City, North Carolina tonight, but the lockmaster termed that "suicidal", quite an overstatement as it turned out.

He also told us that the next lock was 22 miles away, and that the last opening of the day was at 3:30, just four hours away. At six knots, we didn't have time to waste if we wanted to avoid being stuck in the Dismal Swamp Canal for the night. As we left Deep Creek lock, we drove the Gibbous just downstream to a bridge, where we waited as the lockmaster got into his car and drove from the lock to the bridge, where he was also the bridge tender. Now that's efficient staffing! We continued down the Dismal Swamp canal, a scenic run with fall leaves reflecting in the dark waters, stained the color of strong coffee by the rotting leaves forming tannic acid. It was a little surreal, like floating over a black mirror as the beautiful colors reflected in the water.

It was a pretty and calm run, with the only navigating being to keep it in the middle of the narrow channel, and to watch for floating debris. We had a branch go through the props once, but that was all. With not much navigating to do, Captain Rick and I had more time to talk. He'd been complaining since we'd arrived in Maryland about the cold weather, with comments like "Why would anyone live here!", so I was surprised to find out he grew up on a farm in Nebraska. Seems like he'd be used to cold winters.

We somehow got to the bridge before the South Mills lock around 2:30, and we're not sure how we could have gone 22 miles in three hours at the just over six knots we were running. The sailboat Ark had kept pace a little way behind us, and we tied up at the wooden bridge fenders and waited for them to catch up.

Rick called the bridge tender, got the lockmaster who also did double duty, and he informed us he'd be along "directly". I walked up on the bridge to get a few photos of the "Gibbous" in the water, while Capt. Rick went to the other bank to visit with the owners of Ark.

Turned out they had been cruising for two years, and were on their way from Norfolk to their home in St. Petersburg. Rick is from St. Pete also, and we all made plans to hook up for dinner in Elizabeth City that night. We made good time after the canal widened in to the Pasquotank River, and enjoyed the scenery. It's got an isolated look, and a wrecked dive boat beside the channel and the sound of gunshots echoing across the water had us waiting for the banjo music from 'Deliverance" to ring through the trees.

Keeping Us Afloat

As we neared Elizabeth City, we started to see nice waterfront homes, and watched a gorgeous sunset as we approached the lights of the small town. We called Ark on the VHF radio, and they said they were still a few miles behind us, but directed us to the free city slips, where we could tie up and have dinner. They planned on joining us, but darkness overtook them, and they pulled into a small marina short of town. We went through the Elizabeth City Bridge, which opens on demand, and pulled into the slip near dark. We had just missed the party put on whenever new cruisers arrive by the Elizabeth City "Rose Buddies", but we were logged in by Fred Fearing, one of the founders of this welcoming committee.

The town had built new docks in 1983 with 15 free slips to encourage transient boaters to stop and visit the town. Fred and his late friend Joe Kramer decided to welcome the visitors with a wine and cheese party and roses from Joe's garden, and thus the "Rose Buddies" were born. Seventeen years later in 1999, Fred still took his golf cart down to the dock every day to welcome boaters, with wine, cheese and roses donated by local merchants and volunteers. They've greeted as many as 1,000 boats in a single year from as far away as Australia, England, France, Germany and Russia, who come to spend a day or two in this friendly town. Dock slips are free for up to 48 hours, but we would only be using ours for the night.

After a nice dinner at Mulligan's on the waterfront, we made our way out past the sleeping cat in the lounge area, and decided to take a short walk through town. There wasn't much action in town on a Sunday night, but the architecture of the place was certainly interesting. I've always been intrigued by old buildings which would be priceless in a larger town, but which molder away in the undeveloped small towns that spawned them. Here we found a beautiful cast iron fronted building, abandoned and awaiting rescue, it's National Register of Historic Places plaque the only effort that had been made to save it from turning to dust. It looked like a pre 1900 bank, and I once again wanted to take it and move it to our home in Greenville, South Carolina, where it would be a jewel on Main Street. My wife Jenny and I had our photography studio there in a 1929 era synagogue, complete with a dome in its 20 foot ceiling, so we appreciate the effort it takes to save old buildings. This one would have to wait awhile longer for salvation.

Captain Rick and I made our way back to the city docks, checked the lines on the boat, and turned in early at 9:30 p.m. The wind picked up through the night, and it was a little chilly as the docks had no electricity, but I stayed warm enough in my sleeping bag. With waiting for the locks and bridges, the slow speed limit and the twists and turns of the channel it had been slow going that day. We'd only made 45 miles, 185 total for the trip so far, and we still had a long way to go. Rick was up several times in the night, checking and retying lines. I slept like a rock.

Chapter Eight

Monday, November 15th

We awoke at 6 a.m., and after getting dressed, I made tea while Captain Rick checked the engines, and we slipped the lines of the Elizabeth City docks to head for Albemarle Sound at 6:45 a.m. Around 8:30 we entered the Sound for what I thought should have been an uneventful passage in wide open but windy waters. Later I found out how wrong I was. Winds around 25mph had created two to three foot seas that were pounding us around. It was almost impossible to hold a course, cabinets were popping open below, and it took two hands to hold onto the wheel of the boat as we pitched on the waves.

Albemarle Sound gave way to the Alligator River, but offered no relief from the wind and waves.

At 12:30 we raced a couple of sailboats for lead position as we entered the Alligator - Pungo Canal. They would likely be slower than the Gibbous, and hard to pass in the narrow canal. Finally, calm water! We took advantage of the break from rolling to fix soup for lunch, and to grab quick naps in shifts. We passed a swing bridge on the canal, and the bridge tender made us wait until 1:30 p.m. for the next scheduled opening. It was only 10 - 15 minutes, and allowed the three sailboats behind us to catch up and make it through.

The wind picked back up as we entered the Pungo River, and from two to four p.m. we slogged through the wind and waves to arrive worn out at Bellhaven, North Carolina. We checked into the River Forest Manor marina, where we found a local shipyard that carried the fuel filters we needed for 'the Gibbous'. The marina golfcarts were handy for the half mile drive there, and along the way we saw numerous houses being jacked up and new foundations being put underneath. Flood damage only pays two claims per house according to Rick, so FEMA was loaning money to raise the houses before the next series of hurricanes.

We met a kid at the marina whose parents had just moved their family of five aboard a sailboat and were headed for Florida. They weren't sure where in Florida, and the boy sounded envious of our powerboat, saying it looked dryer and warmer. Laundry done and freshly showered, we tried the buffet at the manor house. The food didn't live up to its surroundings.

During dinner Captain Rick struck up a conversation with

our waitress, asking her why anyone would want to live in this cold, isolated place. She said she had grown up here, married her logger husband at the age of 18, and was working towards being a crabber. She didn't sound too happy about it, but she told us she felt she had no other skills and no options. Her husband was 28, had been married before, and spent his evening watching 'wrassling' on TV. Rick had her about half convinced to run away to Florida and get a job cleaning boats, but we didn't see her again, and she'll probably spend her days crabbing. We turned in at 10, ready for an early day Tuesday. We had traveled 79 miles that day, 264 total in four days.

It was nine days until Thanksgiving, and we still had more than 1,000 miles to go.

I lay in my sleeping bag that night thinking about our waitress's sad tale of her limited prospects for the future. Spending your life doing something you don't enjoy sounded like a terrible fate to me. My folks had always encouraged me to find the thing I wanted to do, not to just drift into a career by default. In college, I'd started out wanting to be a lawyer. My run in with the legal system soured me quickly on that, and when I returned to school after getting married, I entered the psychology program at the University of Georgia. My goal was to be a clinical psychologist, and I thought it would be a natural fit for me. My friends and family had frequently turned to me for advice on life and relationships over the years, and the idea of being a counselor sounded appealing.

Unfortunately, the reality of the classroom wasn't the same as the career I had imagined. I got bogged down in the sciences and languages, and even the psychology classes themselves weren't meeting my expectations. We'd spend hours in class discussing one point of view, then the professor would finish with "and that's one of many theories." The lack of absolutes was frustrating. I started looking at other career options, and Journalism began to look appealing. It was not long after the days of Woodward and Bernstein writing about the Watergate scandal, and "All the President's Men" was playing at the theaters.

I decided to give journalism a try.

School had never been easy for me, with brief flashes of success in high school and college that then sank back into my usual academic struggles. Journalism 101 changed all that. It was fascinating to me, and I soaked it up like a sponge. The weekly quizzes were easy, because I was absolutely enthralled with the material we were studying. After the teacher applied his curve to the class, my average was 107 out of 100. I was having fun, and when I made the Dean's list with straight A's, my parents were both shocked and thrilled. Most of my non-major classes were behind me, so I was taking almost exclusively journalism courses.

It had taken me over three years to get through my first two years of college, but I would finish the last two in a year and a half.

My initial goal was to be a writer for specialty magazines, and I decided as part of that goal that I should learn how to take pictures. A camera was a necessity. I didn't have any money for one, but I did have my Ludwig drum set. I'd played drums all through high school, but in spite of my families' belief in me, I wasn't very good. I had great rhythm, but slow hand speed. I'd just never been very coordinated, which led to my always being picked last for the elementary school teams at recess. Reluctantly, I sold my drum set to a kid in a gospel group, bought a used 35mm camera from a friend, and started shooting photos around campus.

I called the school paper, The Red and Black, and asked what it would take to be on their photo staff. They told me to come in and they'd give me an assignment to see how I did. I asked "Does someone process your film for you or do you have to do it yourself?"

The student on the phone chuckled at my naive question and said "No, we're all kind of busy around here, you have to process your own film."

I thanked him, hung up, and went looking for a beginning photography class to sign up for.

The class wasn't easy, and I wasn't a star student. The teacher appeared to have divided us into three groups in his mind, those who were just there for a grade, those who worked hard but weren't very talented, and those with natural artistic genius. I was in the middle group. I got an A, but only by doing an extra credit project. By the end of the class I was shooting and processing my own film, and I was hooked. I spent the summer working for my photography teacher in the Educational Resource Center, processing hundreds of rolls of color and black and white film shot by the university teaching staff. I also mounted thousands of slides, using a semi automatic machine that still required every slide to be handled multiple times. I'll always remember that I was in the midst of an 8,000 slide batch when I heard the news over the radio that Elvis had died at Graceland.

During the summer I also entered a few photo contests, with mixed success. Then I entered the Nikon/Nutshell Magazine Photo Contest, and won a third place. Since there were less than a hundred total winners out of 68,000 entries, I was feeling pretty hopeful that I was learning to be a photographer.

Six months after my first call to the Red and Black newspaper, I was back at their office in the Journalism school building for my tryout. The chief photographer sent me out to take photos on campus, and after shooting a bunch of boring shots of students at play, I went to pick up the new state tag for my car at the local DMV. It was the last day of the month, and lines were long, so I shot a photo of that. I turned it in, and it ran on the front page of the next day's paper. Seeing my photo credit on the front page was all it took for me to change my career.

The Red and Black was unusual as college newspapers go. It was a five day a week daily with a circulation of 16,000, and was supported by paid advertising. During my year there, I was the assistant Photo Editor one semester and the Photo Editor the next two. In addition to shooting college football and other university athletics, I photographed Prince Charles' visit to Athens and Atlanta, Muhammad Ali sparring, a visit by Secretary of State

Henry Kissinger, tennis stars Chris Evert and Martina Navritilova, and even got a call to do a shot for Life Magazine. It was a photo of the world's largest hammock, and it never ran, but my new career was off to a fast start.

Things were a lot rockier at home. Jenny left Davison's Department Store and went to work for the university in their accounting offices, and she and I were spending less and less time together. In between traveling for the school paper, classes and working a part time job, there wasn't much free time in my schedule. Jenny was also traveling to dog shows many weekends with our former neighbor Judy. We'd lived next to Judy in the Crawford barrel house for a year, and Jenny was tired of the isolation and the small space.

On our drive from Crawford to Athens every day, we passed a magnificent old brick plantation house. With the tall white columns and magnolias in the front, it was quite a sight located along the highway in the middle of nowhere. One morning, Jenny called me after she arrived at work.

"David, they're having a yard sale at that plantation house. This is the chance to get a look at it!"

I was a history buff myself and loved old architecture, so I promised her I'd stop at their yard sale on the way to work and school. When I did, I got a surprise. The family having the yard sale had been renting the place, and they were moving out. When I asked about the rent and was told it was $90. a month, I should have known there was something wrong. Jenny was delirious over the idea that we could live in a plantation on several acres, and we immediately called the landlord.

He cautioned me that he was going to have to "raise the rent a little", to $100. a month. We were giddy with the news, and started planning our move to what is now known as the Langston-Daniels House.

The house had gas heat, but the propane tank had been removed by the gas company, and we would need to pay a deposit of several hundred dollars to get a new one installed. It was summer, and we thought we'd do OK for the time being, so we moved in. The house was spectacular, but lacked any modern conveniences. Built in 1820, the last update had occurred in the 1930's when electricity and indoor plumbing were added to the house. The hallway was 10 feet wide and went from the front to the back of the house for ventilation. To add an indoor bathroom, they'd simply walled off one end of the hall, and added a sink, toilet and tub. There was no shower.

The kitchen was spacious, having originally been a parlor, and had a fireplace in it that you could have roasted a pig in. The original kitchen had been outdoors, where the cooking was done over open fires. Off the dining room was the butlers pantry, a shelf lined room where the dishes were brought in from the yard in their iron pots and placed into the fine china bowls for serving.

The living room we turned into our bedroom, with its 12 foot ceilings and tile covered fireplace. The fireplaces everywhere but the kitchen had been converted to coal inserts, tiny little metal grates in the walled up fireboxes. We'd brought our wall to wall rug from the barrel house, and our bed sat on it like an island in the middle of the huge room. In spite of the relatively primitive conditions, we loved our new home, and the adventure of living in something over 150 years old.

While we lived there, a group from the Georgia Historical Society sent a photographer to document the home, as they were trying to get it added to the National Register of Historic Places. They said it was the only brick antebellum home in the area, and were pretty confident of its selection to the National Register. (It was placed on the National Register in 1978.) For me the most fun was watching the photographer moving around the rooms and the columned exterior with his Hasselblad camera on a tripod, using a cable release to click off one image at a time. It was my first time watching a professional photographer at work, and it looked like a great career to me.

We had a few wonderful parties for our friends in the months we lived in the old plantation, gathering around the kitchen fireplace drinking beer, playing ping pong in the upstairs bedroom containing nothing but the game table, sitting on the back porch watching my friends smoking pot. I'd just as soon have a beer myself.

Alas, all good things must come to an end. Between the lack of a shower, our dogs' fear of even walking into the back yard which seemed to be teeming with possums, deer, snakes and such scary creatures, and the snake skin which we'd found in an upstairs closet, Jenny's love affair with the house was about over.

Then the weather turn cold as fall approached. I gathered twigs in the yard to burn in the little coal fireplaces, but the only way we could stay warm was to huddle around the larger kitchen fireplace with its roaring fire. Bathing in the tub in the freezing cold wasn't helping. One morning Jenny's dad called to check on us, and found her with teeth chattering as she tried to talk. He promptly sent deposit money and told us to go to Athens and find an apartment with heat!

As much as we'd loved the adventure of the plantation house, heat and hot showers felt like such a luxury that we were happy with our new two bedroom walkup in suburban Athens. It was also nice being near work, friends and shopping instead of making the long drive to Crawford every day. We settled into apartment life as we entered our third year together, but things weren't all peachy. The fun loving girl I married had turned into someone who could only make love when all her personal stars were aligned.

And that didn't happen often. The first year had gone pretty well, but by the end of the second year the stresses of life and my frustration over our diminishing love life were bringing on a lot of arguments.

She'd acquired a Rottweiler puppy from our friend Judy, and the two of them were spending every other weekend at shows with her new prizewinning pup. It was also sucking up a good portion of our income. Every show she had to help with gas, hotel, pay entry fees, meals, and now handler fees of $50. every time our dog went in the ring. I didn't understand why Jenny couldn't just show the dog herself, but she was too nervous, and insisted that a "professional" handler would give little Berenae the best chance of winning. I didn't understand it all, but was glad she'd found something fulfilling to do. I just wished it wasn't so expensive.

Jenny was also starting to get jealous, a side of her I hadn't seen before and one that I REALLY hated. I'd come home late at night, admittedly as late as 2 a.m., from working in the darkroom at the school paper. I was doing both newspaper assignments and school projects, all after working my part time hours on the sales floor at Davison's, and my patience with her suspicions didn't go very far.

"You have a girlfriend, don't you!", she'd scream at me. I didn't, but the facts really didn't matter. There were girls working at the paper, some in the darkroom, and that's all the proof she needed. I didn't think our marriage could get much more difficult, but I was about to see how wrong I was.

David Crosby

Chapter Nine

By late 1977, Jenny and I were fighting like cats and dogs, and we'd only been married three years. The more jealous she became, the angrier it made me. Life wasn't easy at school either. After more than five years of classes, I was way past ready to graduate and start making a living. My last semester had become a heavy load as I tried to cram enough credits in for graduation. I was taking four major journalism courses, all required, and one, Graphics, had a lab twice a week. A last minute class cancellation had left me with no option except to take a five day a week Communications Law class that I could only attend three days a week because of the Graphics lab. The professor needed bodies to make the class viable, and agreed to the reduced attendance provided I NEVER missed one of those three days a week.

Things were going well three weeks into the semester, my

grades were great, and I felt like my college career was winding down at last. So when my friends on the school paper suggested a Mardi Gras trip to New Orleans, it sounded exciting. We were all broke students, and the plan was for six people to make the trip in a Plymouth Duster for $60. apiece. We'd all crash in one hotel room, college style, and that amount would cover the room and the gas for all three days. I didn't think Jenny would like the idea, especially with her jealousy issues, and I told the group it was doubtful I could go. I told her about the trip, and that I had said I wouldn't go, and she surprised me.

"No, you should go on the trip. You know you want to, and if you don't go, you'll just blame me for it. Go!" she said.

I still felt it would come with a price, and said no. Later that afternoon my friends called again.

"One of the group can't make it, and without you we don't have six people. If you can't go, we're canceling the trip. Come on man, this will be great!"

I was torn, but Jenny had been insistent that I should go, so I said yes.

I should have seen it coming, but was surprised at her reaction when I told her.

"What! You're going!? How could you do that!!?"

"Well," I replied, you TOLD me to go."

She shrieked "But you knew I didn't mean it!"

This was the first of many times I'd hear that phrase over the years of our marriage. She'd claim that she was just trying to please me, but that I should somehow be able to differentiate between the times she was just going along and the times she was really OK with something. Sounded like it required a mind reader to me.

Regardless, I'd committed to the trip, and wasn't backing down now. When I asked who else had signed on, things got worse. Three guys and three girls. Oh boy. That looked bad. Never mind that we were all just friends. There were no romances on the staff, and with six people in the same room, it wouldn't have mattered with the lack of privacy. Jenny was envisioning an orgy, and the mix didn't help.

None the less, I was in for the trip.

We left for the eight hour drive to New Orleans, packed like sardines in the Duster. We were all in great spirits, and when we arrived and checked into our slightly seedy hotel, we couldn't wait to see the town.

The first place we went was the old New Orleans Cemetery. In that part of the country the high water table makes ground burials impossible, so they built crypts and mausoleums above ground. Three of us were photographers, and the scenery there was breathtaking. Carved stone angels loomed over iron gates and stained glass windows everywhere we looked. The poor were buried in niches in the brick walls near the gate, but some of the crypts in the main cemetery were spectacular. The most interesting was a large granite structure we stumbled upon. It was surrounded with chain whose links could hold a ship's anchors.

The fence posts were upended cannons, and the newel posts were cannon balls. As we drew closer we saw it was the tomb of soldiers killed in the war of 1812. Wow. We spent a couple of hours photographing the cemetery, and by then the trip was starting to catch up with us. We headed back to the hotel and crashed for a nap. We awoke a few hours later, refreshed and ready for our first look at Bourbon Street.

We drove to the parking area nearest the Mardi Gras parade route, grabbed a beer in a plastic cup and stood and watched the floats go by. It was a new experience for an Atlanta native, watching the costumed Krewes on their dragon floats as they threw colored beads and decorative coins into the crowd. There was lots of alcohol, but we were on our first beer, just getting started for the evening. We'd been told that after the parade passed, everyone joined the procession and followed the floats to the end, where there was a big street party. Sounded like a fun time to us, so as the last float went by, I joined the crowd stepping over the police barricades.

I put my left leg over first, awkwardly, and as I lifted my right leg over I caught my toe on the top, twisting my leg as I fell into the arms of the New Orleans cop on the other side. I was in a lot of pain, and he handed me off to my friends, who helped me to a seat on the sidewalk. "Damn!" I thought, "Twisted my knee!" I leaned against a wall while the throbbing died down, and after about 10 minutes thought I could try to walk. My friends helped me up, and when I tried to put weight on it, I nearly passed out from the pain. "Wow, I sprained it really bad." I said. "I can't walk." My friends lifted me between their shoulders, and said "No problem, we've got you!" They hauled me around Bourbon Street for the next two hours, where we got more and more drunk as my knee got more and more swollen. At one point we got advised by a couple of friendly hookers walking by that I needed to get my wallet out of my back pocket. It apparently made an inviting target for pickpockets as my friends dragged me along the sidewalks.

Finally I couldn't stand the pain anymore, and I asked my friends to take me back to the motel. We were all exhausted and crashed for the night. When I woke the next morning, my knee was swollen to the size of a basketball. I still thought it was sprained, as I didn't see how a small twist and partial fall could possibly break my leg. But at best I needed an ace bandage and crutches, so I got them to drop me off at the New Orleans Charity Hospital, and arranged to meet them at a bar on Bourbon Street later that evening. I had no idea then what I was in for, as I spent the next ten and a half hours in a scene out of a bad movie. As I entered the lobby in a borrowed wheelchair, a cab screeched to a stop in front of the door. Within seconds a wheelchair was being raced across the lobby, with a man running in front of it. A few minutes later, the cab driver emerged from the ER with eyes as big as saucers. "I caught it, I caught it!" he said. A pregnant woman had taken his cab, and he caught the baby as she delivered it wheeling across the lobby.

Incredible, but just the beginning of a strange day.

Next I was taken to the financial services area, where they asked me where I was employed. "I'm a college student", I replied. "Not currently employed." That was all they needed to know. I was treated without charge.

Next was the triage area. I waited a half hour before being seen by a doctor, who said my knee was too swollen to get my jeans off. He and a nurse took scissors and cut them off. A quick look at my knee and he said "We'll need x-rays." They helped me back into the wheelchair, spread a sheet over my lap as they'd destroyed my pants, and wheeled me into the hallway to wait my turn for x-rays. Being in a charity hospital during Mardis Gras is a recipe for craziness, and I saw plenty of it. A man injured in a bar fight was wheeled in on a gurney for stitches, and with no rooms, they worked on him in the middle of the corridor. He was too drunk to be sedated, so two orderlies held him down while the doctor stitched him up as he flailed and fought them.

Across the hall a man shot in the head in a bar fight sat on a bench. The bullet had just grazed him, but he had a bloody bandage on his head and handcuffs on his wrists. He kept wiping the blood off his head and using it to write things on the floor. I was hoping the police weren't far away.

After six hours waiting in the hall with a sheet on my lap, it was finally my turn in radiology. I was wheeled into the x-ray room, and the radiologist said "OK, hop up on the table."

I told him he was a funny guy, that I could barely move.

He helped me onto the edge of the table, and said "Now I need you to lay on the table and roll onto your stomach."

After telling him what I thought of that idea, he assured me it was necessary to get the x-ray. I struggled onto the table, and with a lot of pain, managed to roll onto my chest. My tormentor wasn't through with me.

He said "Now comes the hard part. I need you to get up on all fours, and lift the injured leg off the table. Hold it there and I'll run behind the screen and get the shot."

"Are you crazy?! I can't move my leg at all!" I pleaded, sure he couldn't be serious.

He once again assured me he was, and that it was the only way to get the x-ray. I struggled into position, trying hard not to pass out from the pain. He ran and got the shot, and I collapsed onto the table, panting with the effort it had taken, my knee a throbbing mass. He helped me shakily off the table and back into my wheelchair, sheet across my lap, as I was wheeled into the hallway to await the results.

By this time, it was starting to sink in that my leg had to be broken. OK, I thought, I can deal with it. Put me in a cast and send me home. But I still wasn't prepared for their diagnosis.

After another long wait, the doctor wheeled me into an exam room, and said "Mr. Crosby, your leg is badly broken. You have a crack in the large bone below your knee that is four inches long, and it's split a quarter of an inch. We're going to have to do surgery to put a metal pin in it, and you'll be in the hospital for a week." OK, now I was worried.

"I can't be in the hospital here, I have classes on Monday in Athens" I said. "And my ride back leaves tomorrow!"

The doc did his best to convince me I was endangering the future use of my leg, but I wouldn't be swayed, I had to go back. The doctor had me sign a release stating I was leaving the hospital against medical advice, put my leg in a 14 pound ankle to thigh cast, and turned me over to a cab driver to take me back to the bar in Bourbon Street where I was meeting the rest of my friends. The hospital had also run out of crutches with the madness of Mardis Gras, I was left to try and hobble without them. Trying to get to a Bourbon Street bar in the middle of Mardis Gras on a Saturday night is easier said than done, and after stopping at a pharmacy to get my pain meds filled, the cab made it through the crowds to a spot a block away from the bar my friends had set for our rendezvous point. I stood in the sea of people, trying unsuccessfully to hop without crutches. Finally a couple of big guys took pity on me and carried me to the bar, depositing me at a table to wait for my friends. When they showed up and saw my predicament, they took me back to the hotel.

My call home to Jenny that night was not pleasant. She was cold and distant on the phone, still angry that I'd made the trip that she'd encouraged me to take.

"SO, " she said, "Are you having a good time?"

I replied, "Well, I've had a little problem." (I've always been a master of understatement.)

"What sort of problem?"

"Well, I kind of tripped and fell down."

"Are you hurt?"

"Yeah, I sorta broke my leg."

"What!!?" was her reply.

I gave her the story, and told her I'd be back tomorrow night, but that Monday morning I'd need to see a doctor, that my leg might need surgery. She was pissed off, and not particularly sympathetic. We ended the call, and I was already dreading the long ride home.

We left early Sunday morning, me sitting by the passenger window with my cast wedged up into the wheel well where I couldn't move. It was a long eight hours, riding cramped and uncomfortable, but I was not eager to rush the reception I expected from Jenny. I got a reprieve when I arrived home though, as my Mom from Chicago and my Aunt Martha from Tallahassee had been traveling together in Georgia, and had detoured to Athens when they heard about my accident. Jenny couldn't tear into me with my mother there, and Mom took over my care, finding me the best orthopedic surgeon in Athens. He was the team doctor for the Georgia Bulldogs, and after x-raying my leg through the cast, said he might be able to set it without a pin. That would shorten my recovery time, and cut my hospital stay considerably. I'd already missed one day of classes, including my "unmissable" Communications Law class, and knew my graduation schedule was at risk.

There was only one catch. "I had to x-ray your leg through the cast, since the risk of damage in replacing the cast is too great", explained the surgeon. "That made the image less than clear, and I won't know for certain if we can avoid operating until we have you on the table and prepped. We'll cut the cast off while you're under anesthesia, and I'll either operate or set it then, depending on what we find. You'll know which option I take when you wake up."

I spent the night in the hospital, and was prepped for surgery early the next morning. My Mom, my Aunt Martha and Jenny were all there, and I felt like Jenny hated the attention I was getting for being injured. They wheeled me into the OR, knocked me out, and when I woke up later that day, I was thrilled to find that the surgeon had been able to set my leg without operating.

I spent two more nights in the hospital, and by Thursday was up on crutches and ready to return to classes. The first one I attended was an optional two hour walking tour of the university printing plant. I'd been looking forward to it all semester, and wasn't about to miss it. Because it wasn't a required field trip, less than half the class showed up, and I struggled through it, hobbling on crutches up and down stairs and metal mesh catwalks, watching as the giant presses rolled through pages and pages of printing. The instructor was handicapped, with one leg shorter than the other, and after watching me struggle on crutches through that tour, I became one of his favorite students.

The rest of the semester wasn't much easier. The UGA Journalism School was a four story building, and though less than 20 years old, it had been built without an elevator. My first class was in the basement, and my second one was on the top floor. It took me the entire 15 minutes between classes just to climb the stairs. I was also the chief photographer of the school newspaper, the yearbook, and was taking a photojournalism class, all of which required me to hold a camera while moving around, not an easy task on crutches. I shot some of my assignments from the window of a friend's pickup truck, which seriously limited my angles. I sat on a stool in the darkroom to make prints and process film.

One of the highlights was photographing Secretary of State Henry Kissinger as he gave a speech in the student union. There was a long line to get in, and some of my photographer friends borrowed a wheelchair for me. That got me in the front of the line, and on the front row for the speech. It also nearly got me tackled by the Secret Service. I didn't see it happening, but apparently as I lifted a long lens to my eye and rolled toward the stage to get a close-up, two Secret Service agents rushed to intercept me, thinking I was a threat. At the last minute they saw I was only shooting photos, and my friends were relieved that I wasn't knocked out of my chair.

The last two months of my college career finally were drawing to a close, and I couldn't wait to get to work. I went to the J school placement office, where I was told "We get a photography related job through here once every year or so.

You might want to plan on getting a part time job while you're job hunting."

I told them they didn't understand, that I'd been in school a long time and was ready to work, but they seemed to think I was being unrealistic. So I took matters into my own hands, and started mailing resumes to newspapers around Georgia and nearby states. I was thrilled when I got an interview with the Aiken Standard, a tiny daily paper in a small South Carolina town. I had neglected to tell them in my inquiry letter that I had a broken leg, so they were a little surprised when I hobbled in on crutches, the pants of my one suit stretched tight over the cast.

I told them "Don't worry, this is only temporary, I'll have the cast off before I start work." I thought the interview went well, but I had gotten some really bad advice. I'd read a book about interviewing skills, and it had recommended that you ask questions such as what are the advancement possibilities, when are raises due, what's the vacation policy, practical questions such as that. After the interview I fully expected to be offered the job, and agonized over whether to accept it. I would be the only photographer on staff, and I really wanted someone to mentor me, and to show me the ropes of the business. The choice was made for me though.

I received a letter from the Standard that said "While we are sure you will make someone a fine photographer, we feel you would not be satisfied with our small operation and the salary we can offer". All of my questions had backfired. So much for

'How To' books. I was crushed by the rejection, but kept applying for jobs.

I got an interview in Jonesboro, Georgia, with the News Daily, a small six day a week paper in suburban Atlanta. Once again I showed up on crutches, this time to be interviewed by Bennet George, the senior photographer. He was a little shocked by the crutches, and I assured him the cast would be off before I started. He seemed impressed with my work, and asked "How long have you been doing photography?"

My reply was "Oh, I've been interested in it for many years". True as far as it went, but I didn't want to admit I'd only owned a 35mm camera for 13 months. I had been the rankest amateur, but was so enthusiastic and determined that I'd become pretty accomplished in a short time. Part of my experience included reading over 2,000 pages of photography history and instruction over the past year, and shooting and processing hundreds of rolls of film. Now it was time for a trial by fire.

I got the job, and would be starting in two weeks, as soon as school ended. I was being paid less than the Aiken job offered by $10 a week, but with another photographer to teach me, I was thrilled. The last two weeks of school were a blur, and when Jenny called to tell her folks I had a job, they were stunned.

"What about school?" they asked.

"Mom, he's graduating!" Jenny told them.

Her parents had just assumed my broken leg would set me back a semester, but I was determined not to let it. After the last day of classes, I went to the surgeon to have my cast removed. He was pleased with my progress, and gave me instructions on rehabbing my leg, weakened by two months in a cast. Stupid me, I hadn't factored that in, and was starting my new career the next day!

I had assured Bennet that I would be ready for work, and didn't want to appear handicapped. I drove to Atlanta, and showed up for the paper at 8:30 a.m., ready to work. The first thing he did was take me to the courthouse a block away to get my sheriffs department press ID. I was excited, but struggled to keep up as we walked the block. Then he decided to take the stairs to the third floor press office.v He fairly ran up the stairs, while I painfully tried to keep up. I was sweating and panting as they took my ID photo, but I got through it.

That afternoon my first assignment as a professional photographer was to shoot a high school baseball game. I showed up at the field, found a good vantage point in front of the stands, and went down on one knee to get a better angle, a habit from covering scores of sporting events. I went down on my bad knee, and just kept going, rolling on to my side on the ground in front of the fans seated in the bleachers. Several people rushed out to help me up, but the only thing hurt was my pride. I decided shooting standing was better, and got through the rest of the day without incident.

Being a newspaper photographer was everything I dreamed it would be except profitable. I was pleased when they told me what my annual salary would be. I had only been paid by the hour in other jobs, so an annual salary sounded great. Then I did the math, and realized it was minimum wage. Oh well, this was more like a paid internship than a long term job, and I knew this was just the starting point. One of my duties was to produce a cover story every other week for the Sunday magazine. I would come up with the topic, shoot it, write the story, lay it out and paste it up. Finally, all those classes were paying off.

I was having a ball. Anything that sounded fun, I'd do a story on it. I'd never flown on anything except a commercial jet, so at first I sought out flying stories. I went up to 10,000 feet in a hot air balloon, flew in a glider and in the chase plane towing them, did barrel rolls in a World War Two fighter plane, and flew over Atlanta at dawn in the traffic helicopter. I would have done this job for free!

My relationship with Jenny was only getting worse though. She resented all of the fun I was having. She's a naturally unhappy person, and all of my joyous enthusiasm for my work was just pissing her off. Our love life came to a near halt. It seemed like the only time she was happy was when she went to a dog show with Judy, something that didn't include me. We lived in a small rental house, and she was always wanting more. She had been driving a crappy old Rambler station wagon with a leaky windshield that we'd paid $400. for, and when she got a decent paying job, the first thing we did was buy her a brand new sporty

Mitsubishi with a hefty monthly payment. She always had us living beyond our means, and it was my job to make it work.

It was a struggle that would continue as long as we were married.

Chapter Ten

Tuesday, Nov. 16th

We left the Bellhaven dock at 7 a.m., along with several other transient boats. Aura, a 54 foot Krogen with two sails and a crows nest, took off ahead of us. It's owner Maury Barrett and his wife had been cruising for a while, and seemed surprised when we said we were planning to make Sarasota before Thanksgiving. They were hoping to make Charleston, SC, by Thanksgiving! Most of the folks we met cruising the ditch weren't in a real big hurry. At 8 a.m. the Barrett's put up both sails on their Krogen, a rare sight. We got some good shots and promised to send them a few to their home in Pennsylvania. At 8:15 we left the Pungo and entered the Pamlico River. The river later gave way to a canal, and we bumped the bottom rounding a channel marker. I threw the boat out of gear, but we weren't aground. We continued on, and Capt.

Rick said I handled it exactly right, a nice compliment to this novice captain. We passed a Coast Guard station on the canal, and heard them warn a large cruiser that had blasted past us earlier about obeying the no wake zone. They politely told the captain that he was responsible for his wake, slow it down! It wouldn't be the last time we heard that on this trip.

At 9:45 we entered the Bay River, then the Neuse River. We passed the sailboat Nugget, whom we had last seen in Norfolk. He took the Albemarle Canal because of his deeper draft, and apparently made better time than we did with the Dismal Swamp route. At noon we entered another canal from the Neuse, and watched as a sailboat aground on Adams Point got a tow off. Groundings are pretty common in these shallow waters. We'd heard traffic on the VHF for hours about assisting him, and arrived just as he got free. Running aground is frustrating and expensive, something we wanted to avoid if at all possible. We had planned to stop in Morehead City, but we got there at 2:30, and didn't want to waste the daylight. We called a couple of marinas at Bogue Inlet in Swansboro, but the first one we called told us it was too far to make in daylight.

Casper's Marine told us no problem, it's 25 miles, you should make it, and it's well marked with flashing lights if it gets too dark.

We headed past Morehead City, where the channel is in protected waters and was a nice scenic ride, with New England style cottages and homes lining the waterfront, but the wind and cold started to get tiring. We arrived at Casper's Marine at 4:30 p.m., where I got a semi successful lesson in tying up in a strong current. Capt. Rick took over, not wanting to keep the dock man waiting. Casper's is a family owned marina, and the staff is mostly his family. His father started it, and they've just rebuilt all new facilities after suffering through their third major hurricane in just three years. Unrepaired docks and houses are widespread, but it's a picturesque little place. Casper's grand-daughter drove us to the River View Restaurant, where we got a good dinner of soft shell crab and shrimp, and the owner, John, drove us back to the boat. Great hospitality. I fell asleep at 10 before I could even get undressed, windburned and tired. We had gone 85 miles that day, 349 total for the trip.

Before the wind had picked up in the afternoon, Rick had wanted to hear more about my flying experiences. He'd had a few of his own after all, including being flown out west on a private jet to repair the owner's water heater at his mountain lodge when Rick was the captain of a 103ft yacht.

I'd run out of most of my flying opportunities after a year at the Jonesboro News/Daily, and was ready for greener pastures. I really wanted to get away from Georgia, after spending most of my years living there, so I sent resumes' to small papers all over the country. I think the farthest was in Muskogee, Oklahoma. Wouldn't you know it, the most encouraging response was from Columbus, Georgia, a mid sized newspaper a few hours West of Atlanta. I called them up and spoke to Allen, the assistant chief photographer. He suggested I come visit in a week or two. I said, "How about tomorrow?" I drove to Columbus for the interview, and thought it went well, but when a week went by and I hadn't heard from them, I thought it was time for a nudge. I started calling them regularly, until they just gave up and hired me.

Things got off to a fast start, when after being in Columbus just a few weeks, I was driving in town and saw a large shadow pass over my car.

I looked out the window, and saw it was the Goodyear blimp overhead! I raced back to the paper, determined to find a way to get a ride.

Before I could say a word, the chief photographer said "David, I need you to do something for me. I'm supposed to do a press tour on the Goodyear blimp tomorrow, and I've got a wedding to shoot. I want you to cover it for me."

I quietly agreed, although I felt like cheering.

The next day was as exciting as I expected. I photographed the blimp on the ground, with the ground crew struggling to hold it stable. The blimp doesn't land like an airplane, but has dozens of ropes hanging off of it. While taking off, a dozen men hold the lines, and let go on a signal. When it comes in for a landing, they essentially catch it, grabbing the ropes as they get in reach. As the six of us boarded the gondola, I was surprised by the small size of the cabin. There was a single pilot's seat, with a control like a sideways steering wheel next to it. The wheel actually pivoted the prop engines on each side of the gondola, angling the blimp up or down. The side to side movement was controlled by pedals which moved the rudder vanes on the tail.

The pilot toured us over the city, a slow and stately pace in contrast to the noisy engines. Then he let each of us take turns piloting the blimp. I got to fly it for 10 minutes, getting it tilted down and off course to the left as the pilot took pictures of me flying it. Like I said, things were getting off to a great start in Columbus.

Unfortunately, my satisfaction in my new job didn't last long. At the News/Daily, my first newspaper job, if we didn't have an assignment, we'd better be out looking for something to shoot. That's the way it works at most papers. Not at the Columbus Ledger-Enquirer in 1979 though. Half of the photo staff was near retirement age, and seemed to feel like you shouldn't work more than absolutely necessary. I was 25 years old, ambitious and full of energy, and the boss and especially his assistant Allen felt I was making them look bad.

One of the first weeks I was there, I had three assignments, at 2:30, 3:30 and 4:30 p.m. They were all quick head shots and check presentations, but they were also in the same area about 20 minutes away from the paper. If I'd driven back to the office in between, I would have been at the paper less that five minutes before I had to drive back again. I had a company car, but it sure didn't seem like the best use of my time or the gas for the car, so I went to a nearby park where I shot feature pictures of kids playing in between the assignments.

Arriving back at the paper before 5 p.m., when I walked in, Allen said "Where the hell have you been?!"

I was a little mystified by this, and explained to him what the timeline and my thinking about it was, and told him I had several feature pictures from the park.

"Nobody told you to do that!" was his reply.

This was the beginning of a nearly two year battle for my sanity at the Columbus paper.

The editors loved my taking the initiative to do extra work, but it kept me constantly in the doghouse with my photo department bosses. One of the worst was when I found out that a major Hollywood film, 'The Long Riders', was being filmed an hour and a half away in tiny Parrott, Georgia. The producers had rented the town for a month, covering the paved main street with twenty boxcar loads of Louisiana sand to make it look like Northfield, Minnesota. It was the story of the James gangs raid on Northfield, and was being made with three sets of brothers, David and Keith Carradine, Randy and Dennis Quaid, and James and Stacy Keach. One of our paper's reporters had gotten a job as an extra on the film, and was writing a daily column on his adventure. The only problem was that he wrote for the small North Georgia edition of the Ledger-Enquirer. The folks in Columbus knew nothing about Hollywood being on their doorstep.

It seemed like a great opportunity, but I knew that my boss

would simply take the assignment for himself if I told him about it. Instead, I had the reporter get me a press pass, and for three days I left at 8 a.m. for Parrot, Georgia, shot on the set for half a day, then drove back to Columbus in time for my 2 to 11 p.m. shift. By the end of the week I was exhausted, but I'd had fun shooting the stars and looking behind the scenes of a Hollywood film. I gave the prints to the city editor, who ran a front page story and photos, with a picture page inside. I also sold several to the Associated Press wire service, which published them across the country. A great success, and I was in trouble at work for a month! I did it on my own time, but that didn't matter. In the bosses' eyes, I had shown him up.

Every time I did something on my own initiative, I got in trouble. Being on the bosses sh*t list meant I didn't get choice assignments, so I had to be careful. Fortunately there was only one other person on my 2-11 p.m. shift, and that was Joe Maher. Something of an aggressive curmudgeon, Joe was in trouble as often as I was, and they couldn't deny both of us the best assignments when we were the only ones there to shoot them. That meant the plum jobs went to who ever was in the least trouble that week. We were also the two best photographers, and that seemed to irritate the boss even more.

The next episode was the firemen's Olympics, a sort of field day for area firefighters. They did ladder races, barrel rolls where they used hoses to roll barrels across the finish line, and the finale, where they had a tug of war. In that event there was a barrel suspended with a pulley on a wire between two telephone poles, and competing teams tried to blast it to the other side against each other with their fire hoses. It made for great visuals, and I wanted to make the most of it.

The event lasted for three hours, and I had looked to make sure there was nothing else on the schedule at the paper before I left. When I'd been there just a half hour, I heard the familiar whiny voice of Allen, the assistant chief, asking where I was. This was in the days before cell phones, and we had walkie talkies to communicate. They were limited in range, and so I answered by turning the squelch up and down a few times, telling him "I can't read you", and then turning the radio to off. I knew I'd pay a price for it, but the best images were yet to come.

Arriving at the paper 15 minutes after the event ended, I was greeted by Allen's usual "Where the HELL have you been?!"

I told him, "The event was three hours long, and I left as soon as it was over."

"Nobody told you to stay for the whole thing!" he yelled at me.

I asked, "Did you need me for something else?"

"That's not the point!" he fumed. It was Life in Columbus.

I finally got so frustrated with being yelled at all the time for working hard, that I decided to try an experiment. I told my wife Jenny, "I'm going to be just as lazy as they are, doing nothing beyond the bare minimum. See how they like THAT!" For weeks I did as little as possible. I'd race out to do my assignments, snap a few quick shots, and race back to the paper to process them. As soon as the prints were captioned and turned in, I parked my butt in one of the chairs in our bullpen area, and waited for someone to tell me to do something.

The editors asked me "What's wrong with you?" I couldn't really explain that I was testing my bosses. I thought the bosses wouldn't like it, and I knew the editors wouldn't.

Much to my surprise, in the third week of my experiment, Allen told me "I'm glad to see you settle down and become one of us. I knew you'd fit in eventually and become a good staff photographer."

After four weeks, it was making me crazy to do nothing. I was irritable at home, and knew I was producing nothing of value. And it wasn't having the desired effect. My immediate bosses loved my new attitude!

Finally my wife had enough. "Go back to work, this is making you crazy, and you're making ME crazy!"

And she was right. So I resigned myself to being constantly in trouble, and went back to my old way of working.

Sometimes the challenge at work was just dealing with deadlines. Joe and I took turns shooting football games for the Alabama editions of the newspaper, and as soon as we crossed the border the time zone was an hour earlier. I'd drive an hour and a half to a high school in Alabama for a game with a 7:30 start time. That meant it was 8:30 Georgia time. The deadline to turn in the photos was 10 p.m., and I had an hour and a half drive to get back.

So after the long drive, I'd shoot the kickoff, run to the car and race back to the paper. On arriving I'd develop the black and white film in heated developer to cut the time down, place it for 30 seconds in the fixer, just long enough to stop the development and then swish it in the rinse waters for about 15 seconds. Then I'd edit the wet negatives, put it in the enlarger and print it wet. Less than 10 minutes after my return, the editor had a print. Whew. It wasn't high art, but the challenge of making things work in seemingly impossible circumstances was great fun.

On one interesting day at the paper, I saw a crew working on the five story steeple of a historic church in the town. The workers were sandblasting the sides of the brick tower, and I thought it would make great visuals. After clearing it with the construction foreman, I climbed a 100 year old three story ladder to access the rooftop work area. It was a difficult climb, with the rickety ladder shaking as I made my way up it, heavy camera bag hanging from my shoulder and a steady stream of fine sand falling into my face from above. It was playing havoc with my contact lenses, and I made much of the climb with my eyes closed.

At the top, there were safety fences all around the steeple tower, with an opening on one side where the worker doing the sandblasting hung from cables as he worked. I wanted to shoot that angle, and the only way to do it was to lean out over the edge. No one ever believes me when I tell them I'm actually afraid of heights, but it was a scary moment as I leaned as far as I could over the edge of that high tower, a construction worker holding my belt from behind to keep me from toppling over. It made a great shot, but when I came home and told my wife how I got the picture, she said "We need to increase your life insurance!"

Meanwhile, life with Jenny was not getting any easier. She had found a job at Aflac but hated it, and quit after a few months. I couldn't really blame her for that one though. She would come home every night depressed, but wouldn't say what was bothering her. Finally one night she burst out crying and said "I read autopsy reports all day!" Turns out her job was to verify that claimants had died of cancer, so she spent the days reading vivid accounts of the sights and smells of the dead and their internal organs. Not something suited to her temperament.

She found another job as a bookkeeper at a department store, and was at least able to help keep up with her car payments. She really just didn't like working. We hardly saw each other, with her working daytime 9-5 hours, and me working Tuesday through Saturday, 2 to 11 p.m.

Sunday was our only real day together. She started hanging out with friends from her office who liked to frequent the hotel bars after work. One evening when I came home after 11 p.m., she still hadn't returned, and I went to bed, knowing she was out with friends. When I was awakened at 2 a.m. by the front door shutting, I was surprised by the time as I looked at the clock. Jenny stumbled into the bedroom, having left a trail of clothes from the front door to the bed. She flopped on the bed naked, and promptly rolled off onto the floor. I helped her back into bed, but it wasn't long before she was in the bathroom, giving up the night's drinking to the toilet.

The story I heard the next morning was that it was ladies night at the bar, and a table of guys kept sending them drinks. She and her friends got plastered, and when she started to drive home, she took a right turn instead of a left from the hotel parking lot. She drove 80 miles in the wrong direction before she discovered her mistake. God truly watches out for drinkers sometimes. This was highly unusual behavior for Jenny, but it was a sign of her deepening unhappiness. Many weekends she was off on the dog show circuit with her friend Judy, where she was showing our rottweiler. This included travel and hotel costs, entry fees and $50. a shot every time a handler took our dog in the ring. This was not a hobby for people on our kind of budget. Her goal was to get our dog Berenae a champion title, which required winning her class in a certain number of shows. The more shows she went to, the better her chances. And the bills mounted.

Between the frustrations of my job at the newspaper and Jenny's ever increasing need for me to make more money, I pondered where my career was leading me. My University of Georgia Journalism degree had helped me get two jobs already, but I wondered if an advanced degree might move things along and lead to jobs in bigger markets. I looked into grad school, and settled on either Rochester Institute or the University of Missouri Journalism School. Both had fine photography programs, and I thought they might accelerate my career.

I needed to take the Graduate Record Exam for my application, and called the company that administers it to find out when it was next offered in my area. It was Friday, and I found out that it was being offered Saturday, the very next day. Not knowing any better, I signed up over the phone with a credit card, and showed up the next morning for the test. I felt like it went pretty well, and was pleased a few weeks later when my score came in the mail. It would be more than enough to help my admission prospects. Later I was to find out that most people study for months before taking the GRE. I'd always done well on standardized tests, and not knowing any better probably helped me to be relaxed.

My Mom was always up for a road trip, so she and I piled into the car and drove to Rochester, New York. I met with the officials in the Photography program at RIT, and got disappointing news. Their program was highly technical, including the chemistry for film and development. My liberal arts degree wouldn't be enough, I would need to get another degree from RIT before I could even start the grad program. Since I was only planning to devote a year to this project, RIT was out of the running.

Mom and I made a detour to visit Niagara Falls, where we rode the 'Maid of the Mists' boat under the spray of the falls, and I used an old Speed Graphic camera from the 1940's to shoot 4x5 negatives of the roaring waters from the opposite cliffs. It was always fun traveling with Mom.

Then it was on to Columbia, Missouri. There I toured the school, and met with the Photojournalism programs famous director, Angus MacDougall. McDougall had literally written the book on the current state of the art of photojournalism, and I was thrilled to meet with him. He asked when I was thinking of coming to school, and I said "Next semester."

He replied "That starts in less than a month, it's way too late to get accepted now."

He was surprised when I told him I'd stopped by admissions on the way in. I'd already been accepted. Between my GRE score, my college grades, and my life experience as a working photojournalist, they'd decided that I was a good candidate for the grad program.

We spent the next hour talking about my goals in coming to Missouri, and I told him about the depressing situation I was in with the paper in Columbus.

He surprised me when he said "The graduate program isn't really about making you a better photographer. It teaches you about editing, managing people, using photography to tell stories, and layouts and design. It's really aimed at becoming department heads and photo editors. You don't need grad school, you just need a better job!"

This wasn't what I expected to hear. I thanked him and left, needing to make a quick decision. I returned to Columbus, where the plan had been for Jenny to stay there and work while I lived in a dorm at Missouri.

We expected to be able to visit each other every couple of months.

First I thought I could do it in a year, then it started to look like eighteen months, possibly up to two years.

Jenny said "I may not be here when you get back if you're gone that long."

So I put my continuing education plans aside, and started looking for a better job. Once again I sent my resume' all over the country, and again the best leads were closer by. I interviewed with the Associated Press in Atlanta, and while they liked my work, they didn't think I had enough experience for the position. The editor suggested Greenville, South Carolina, a place I'd never been, and offered to put in a good word for me with the chief photographer.

It wasn't so far away from Atlanta, but at least it was in another state. I called and arranged an interview, was hired quickly and within weeks we were moving to Greenville.

Chapter Eleven

Wednesday, November 17th

Captain Rick and I were up at 5:30 a.m. today, ready to make a long run. I got a lesson in pulling away from the dock at Caspar's in a current, and as we were only four or five feet from the sailboat docked ahead of us, Rick was watching me closely. We headed down the ICW as a beautiful sunrise was just building. At 7:40 a.m. we went through the Onslow Beach swing bridge with a couple of sailboats. A swing bridge is quite a sight, as the entire structure pivots 90 degrees from the center, giving boats two sides to go through. The bridge is manned by the US Marines as it's part of a firing range on the ICW. We had seen signs that if there were red flags and yellow flashing lights, the ICW was closed for gunnery practice. We also had a couple of Marine boats zoom past us and wave.

One of the sailboats we passed was "Flying Low" a boat that had been docked next to us at Bellhaven. He'd been running long days to keep pace with us, as our eight and a half knots was more than he could manage. We took a few shots of his boat, and promised to send skipper Harold Graul a print. At 8:55 we went under the fixed bridge at Goose Bay. At 9:30 I called my Dad, and Capt. Rick and I sang Happy Birthday to him over the cell phone. I was really looking forward to making it back in time to spend Thanksgiving with my family in Greenville.

At 10 a.m. we sat and waited 20 minutes for the Sears Landing swing bridge to open, as it has an hourly schedule. We were starting to get tired of all the no wake zones and bridge delays that are part of traveling the Intra Coastal Waterway. It's a tough trip to make as fast as we were attempting it. We passed a lot of clam beds with orange "Closed to Clamming" signs on them because of health concerns, and quite a few them had people in the water harvesting the tasty shellfish anyway, as many as three people at once in one closed area. Near lunchtime we passed Wrightsville Beach, an area I'd vacationed in with my family the previous year with our Hobie Jet runabout. It was fun to pass through on the 'Gibbous' the areas we had puttered around in before, including the beached sailboat I had explored with my young nephew Russell out on the sand island. When we'd been there the past year, I'd watched the boats passing through on the ICW, jealous of their freedom and never dreaming that I'd be making the trip myself so soon.

Next came the Cape Fear River, a large body of water that included ship traffic, a naval demolition vessel passing us, and a Navy SEAL team training local law enforcement in diving techniques. After the Cape Fear River we went through SouthPort, a very picturesque place, definitely worth a visit. Holden Beach down the channel was also a quaint looking community, and very close to the beachfront. Just after sunset we arrived at the Pelican Pointe Marina at Tubbs Inlet, where the owner came back after closing to fuel us up.

He'd started life as a CPA, and bought the marina ten years ago to spend his time on the water. He was envious of our trip, saying he'd never gotten a chance to run the ICW. Now the area has gotten so crowded with beach homes and tourists that he was selling out, and planned to move to the mountains where he could be around fewer people on more land. It must be strange to talk with so many people passing through your little piece of the Intra Coastal Waterway, and yet never make the trip yourself. After putting in a couple of hundred gallons of diesel, he dropped us off at a restaurant about 10 minutes away. We had a good clam dinner, hopefully from safe clam beds, then caught a ride back to the marina with a kitchen worker on her way home. I was always impressed with how everyone seemed willing to help traveling boaters.

As we'd enjoyed the scenery on the day's run, Captain Rick had wanted to hear more about my life and marriage. After taking the job in Greenville, my boss had given me a map of the area, circling the areas that were safe to live in and affordable. We'd looked at many houses, because with two dogs and a cat we didn't feel an apartment would work. We found a nice 1930's era bungalow, and returned to Columbus to start packing. I drove an elderly VW bus at the time, and as we couldn't afford to hire movers, we moved most of our belongings in my bus. It made for a slow process, making lots of five hour trips back and forth.

As things piled up in the new home while Jenny remained in Columbus, I spent the night at our new home, got a take out dinner, and sat down to watch TV. Hmmm, where did I put that TV set? After looking all through the house for our small portable TV, I noticed the footprints on an unlocked window in the living room. We'd been robbed! I searched the house, but couldn't find anything else missing. What a lousy way to be greeted in our new home. I chalked it up an opportunistic thief, made sure all of the windows were locked, and on the next trip brought our dogs, thinking they might deter would be thieves.

We barricaded our fuzzy black dogs Christopher and Carly in the kitchen, left them food and water and headed back for another trip. When we returned late at night, I saw immediately that the porch light was out. I knew I'd left it on. We rushed into the house to check on our pets, who were happy and unharmed in the kitchen. They may have barked at the returning burglars, but they sure didn't slow them down. This time they'd broken a window to get in, and taken everything of value that they could carry. Stereo, antique cameras, all of my tools, my slide projector, this time we'd been cleaned out.

Jenny was too scared to live there after being robbed twice in a week, so we went to the landlord and demanded to be let out of the years lease. Under the circumstances, he didn't put up much argument. We found a home in Easley, a small town 20 minutes from Greenville, and started moving again. By the time we were settled in, I was exhausted after two moves in two weeks.

Meanwhile, I started my new job at the Greenville News. It was largest paper I'd worked for, with seven shooters on the photo staff. There was a lot to learn, including handling lighting on location and in the paper's small studio. When I started, one of my first assignments had been to photograph a couple of models with a Christmas tree for a Sunday Magazine cover. The boss said "Take the lights". When I was hired, he'd asked if I was familiar with using lights, and I said I was. What I didn't say was that I was familiar with continuous quartz lighting, and these were strobes, a whole different thing. I'd never used a flash meter, and had no idea how to measure the light output. I took the lights on the shoot, arranged the models and proceeded to shoot slides at every f stop setting on the camera, figuring one of them had to be right! It got me through the assignment, and when I returned to the paper I asked one of the other photographers for a lesson on using the strobes and the flash meter.

I had a lot of fun at my new job, shooting the Master's golf tournament in Augusta, major college sporting events, and news around the region. At the time the News was the best paper in the state, and I was proud to be working there. After working in Columbus where I felt like I was being held back by my bosses, this was a new experience. In the first month, I was one of three photographers, including my boss George, who got the call to cover a large house fire. The fire spread to the house next door, and I stayed to look for interesting angles while my co-workers headed back to the office. When I returned, their shots were already turned in to the city editor. I printed an artsy shot of the S shaped curve of the hose leading to the firemen, silhouetted in the smoke between the two houses as they struggled against the blaze. I took it to George, and he grabbed it and walked to the city editors desk.

He said "Give me those fire pictures I handed you a little while ago." The editor looked confused, but gave them back to him. George handed him my shot and said "Run this one."

I was so impressed! What a change from the jealous and backstabbing ways of the Columbus Ledger-Enquirer. (The fire photo went on to win best news photo of the year in the state Associated Press awards.)

I was loving my work, but as usual, Jenny wasn't happy. She searched for a while, and found a bookkeeping job at a struggling textile company. The textile business had once been the bedrock of Greenville's manufacturing industry, but as textile manufacturing all moved overseas for the low labor cost, it was dwindling fast. That job was typical of her work history. She'd start a new job, and after a year or two leave for something else. Nothing seemed fulfilling for her, and she was envious of how much I enjoyed my work. Jenny also had a dismal outlook on life, fearful and expecting the worst. My sunny disposition got on her nerves, and she called me "Pollyanna" after the perennially cheerful character in a Disney movie.

How dare I be so damn happy all the time!

Jenny moved from textiles to a bookkeeping job at a blueprint company, and eventually to running their small central office computer for them. She seemed to be down all the time, something that I only realized later was a series of depression episodes. Nothing ever seemed to make her happy, except spending money. Jenny always wanted something new, a new house, a new car, new clothes, new dog, always something she didn't have. Trying to make her happy was a never ending job, but one that I believed was my responsibility.

When a personality conflict at the blueprint company job led her to quit in anger, I was tired of the jobs merry go round, and tired of being the only one having any fun. I told her "Jenny, I could teach you to be a wedding photographer, and with your artistic background, I know you'd be a success!"

She responded that she hated weddings, and I asked her what she would like photographing. She said "pets".

So I said "Fine, we'll make you a pet photographer." Jenny was skeptical, but I knew I could teach her if she wanted to do something fun for a change. I loaned her one of my Nikons, and started teaching her the basics.

We quickly discovered that me teaching her was like teaching your own teenager to drive. They don't listen, and it becomes a frustrating experience for both of you.

So I signed her up for a beginning photography class at the Greenville Museum School, and she quickly became a star pupil. Of course, Jenny had a few advantages over the rest of the students. She'd been watching me at work for several years, she had access to any equipment she needed, and while her classmates fought for darkroom time at the small museum facility, she came to the newspaper at night and used the Greenville News darkroom to work on her projects. By the end of class, she was taking photos of peoples pets for money, and soon set up a small corner in a friend's pet store to sell her services.

That only worked out for a while, and I spent the summer building a full darkroom and small studio in the basement of our house for her to use. I learned carpentry, wiring and plumbing in the process, doing all of the work myself. By the fall she was ready to start taking clients at the home studio, but seemed to have a problem with getting motivated. Her lack of self-confidence had always been a problem for her, and now it was keeping her from making any money at her new profession. Plus, her desire for more and better things still ruled her. She decided that she could do better work if only she had a medium format camera. We didn't have the $1,800. that it cost at the time to get her a Bronica

645 with lens and film back, so it was up to me to find a way. I ended up selling my 18 foot ski boat so she could have the camera she wanted. I used to hold the camera in one hand, and tell people "Look, this is my boat!"

Still she struggled to get clients. And so I found another way for her to get photography experience. I was acquainted with Blake, a Greenville commercial photographer, and knew he sometimes hired assistants. I went and spoke with him, and he agreed to give Jenny a try. The pay wasn't much, but she could earn a little bit while learning the ropes of the photography business. She was thrilled! For a while she loved it, but as usually happened with Jenny, after a year or so she started to feel unappreciated and dissatisfied. She decided she was going to quit, and didn't show up for a scheduled shoot. When Blake called the next day and fired her for not showing up, she was hysterical. "I've never been fired before!', she wailed. I didn't understand why she was so upset, since she was quitting anyway, but that was the way things worked with Jenny.

The biggest advantage to Jenny's brief employment with a commercial photographer was the chance to see what the business was like, how people charged for it and what was required. It didn't take Jenny long to suggest that I could do a better job of it than her boss. One day while she was still employed at his studio, Jenny came home and said that Blake, her boss, wanted me to do a shoot for him. He had a regular customer, a company that made controls for nuclear power plants, and they had a panel that was about to be shipped and needed to be photographed. Blake had a more lucrative job out of town that day, and decided I should cover for him with his other client. I was a little irritated that he didn't ask me, he just told Jenny "Have David shoot it."

I was scheduled to work at my newspaper job the next day at 2 p.m., so I had a limited amount of time to do the project. When I arrived at the plant the next morning, I discovered that the panel was fourteen feet long and seven feet tall. The client wanted it photographed with all of the panels lit and working, which meant we had to get the lighting and camera set, and then shoot the images during the factory lunch hour when we could turn out the overhead lights in the plant and light up the panel. That didn't leave a lot of time to get the photographs done, get the gear packed and still make it to my newspaper shift at 2 p.m.

We worked fast, and had everything ready for when we could go lights out in the factory. By the time we were done shooting, I was running out of time and had to leave Jenny to pack up the gear. Blake wanted me to deliver the film to him and let him deliver it with the bill to his client so that they wouldn't know it didn't come from him. I didn't mind that, but was still annoyed that he had assumed I would do the shoot without asking. I told Jenny that I thought I should get any fee for the shoot, and that I planned to tell Blake that was what I wanted. He was famous for his violent temper, and Jenny said "I don't want to be there when you tell him that!" I had a break at work at the News, and told my boss I was walking down the street to Blake's studio to discuss my fee with him.

When I arrived and told Blake that I wanted to be paid whatever he normally charges, he went ballistic.

His face turned red, and he started thumping his chest and saying "MY day rate! You want to charge MY day rate!? Do you know how many years it took me to earn that? That's MY day rate!"

I simply replied, "I did the shoot, I should get the fee. If you wanted to negotiate something less, you should have asked me instead of just telling Jenny to have me DO the shoot."

He reluctantly agreed to my terms, but was definitely not happy about it. When I returned to the newspaper, my boss George asked how it had gone.

"Well" I replied, "I haven't been called a motherf**ker since high school!"

My work at the Greenville News-Piedmont was becoming more and more frustrating. My boss who started out so inspirational had become something of a tyrant.

He proudly boasted that when the executive editor had made him the chief photographer he'd told George it was because "You're the only one in the building who is as big of an S.O.B. as I am."

That sure didn't seem like something to brag about. I wasn't a brown noser, and was prone to speaking up when I was unhappy about something, which had led to a few clashes with George.

Part of my problem with photojournalism was the idealism I carried with me from my days in the University of Georgia's Journalism program. The integrity and search for the truth that was drilled into us at school seemed a foreign concept in the real world of advertisers and office politics. I felt like this was MY work, not the newspaper's, which didn't always make me the best employee.

Newspapers are run by writers, who then become editors. Rarely is someone with a photographic or visual background in charge of anything more than other photographers. Frequently our names would be left off the credit line of a photo. No matter how bitterly I complained, it was always chalked up to simple error. That would be easier to believe if even ONCE a writer's credit line had been omitted.

One episode really made it clear to me. The Russians had shot down a Korean passenger airliner that strayed into its air space, killing all aboard. If there's one thing that local newspapers love, it's a national story on their doorstep. One of the passengers killed was Benny Hong, a golf pro at a Greenville area course. There were only a few Americans on board, so when the family held Hong's memorial service on the 18th green of Bonnie Brae golf club, over 500 people showed up for the service, including more than a hundred national and international journalists. I covered it for our papers, and got a dramatic shot of Hong's mother kneeling in front of his widow flanked by her children, patting her knee with the widow wiping a single tear away from her face.

I proudly delivered it to the News city editor for inclusion in the morning paper, confident it would make page one. When the editor came back to me a few minutes later asking me to print another image, one where the widow was not crying, I was stunned. "What's wrong with the one I gave you?" I asked.

The city editor said "Tom (the managing editor) doesn't want us to invade her privacy."

I was flabbergasted. I told him "How can I invade her privacy in front of 500 people and press from around the world?! That's just stupid. She's the one who held such a public memorial!"

The editor was pissed off at me for blasting him, and insisted on getting a non-crying photo. I thought it was dishonest, as she had cried through most of the service, and the boring photo where she was composed did not represent the truth to me. When I was on the way out that evening after work, I ran into Tom, the managing editor who'd killed my shot, in the hallway approaching the elevator.

Tom was not one for mingling with his staff, particularly the photographers, and I was surprised when he said "Hi David, how are you?"

He was not expecting my reply.

"Well Tom, I'm not too good. You killed my shot from the memorial service because it would invade the widow's privacy.

How the heck do you invade someone's privacy on the 18th hole of a golf course in front of 500 people?"

He looked shocked at my outburst and said "David, decisions are made at the editorial level that you might not understand."

He might as well have slapped me. I shot back "Tom, I have my journalism degree just like you do!"

He stuttered and stammered that if I had a complaint, I should go through channels and talk to my boss. Tom was my boss's, boss's boss.

Fortunately there was no fallout from my outburst, and the Piedmont, the afternoon paper, ran my photo on the front page the next day. They thought Tom's concerns were just as ridiculous as I did. But I was getting sour on the Greenville News Piedmont. I loved my work, but was rapidly losing respect for the institution and my employers. In the past, my career goals were to keep moving to bigger and better newspapers, and then onto national magazines, where I could travel the world. After attending numerous seminars where nationally known photojournalists spoke, the reality of their lives was less appealing to me. It involved being gone many months each year, and a lot of them were single or divorced. Their friends were the other journalists they traveled with. I had gotten attached to Greenville and it's slower pace, and while I loved New York City in small doses, I just couldn't see myself living their lifestyle. I didn't want to leave my family behind either. Jenny was frequently difficult to live with, but I didn't like the idea of months away from her.

So what was I going to do?

Jenny began encouraging me to start a commercial photography business, but we had no savings, and no way to live while we got it off the ground. Jenny's former boss Blake had a contract to provide publications photography to nearby Furman University, and I had filled in out there for him several times when he had a conflict. The staff liked me, and when they told me that Blake was thinking of resigning the contract, I told them I would be interested in the job if he left. The contract renewed every fall, and I spent a nervous summer waiting to see if he would go. When he finally announced his departure, I gave my 30 day notice to the Greenville News Piedmont, and started planning my new career, happy to be on my own at last.

Chapter Twelve

Thursday, November 18th

It was an early morning, getting up at 5:30, and we departed Pelican Pointe at 6:15 a.m. before sunup. Soon after getting underway we went under my first pontoon bridge, a strange contraption where the roadway is actually on a barge which is swung out of the way of the channel on cables powered by a diesel winch. Before this trip I'd never been through a lock or had a bridge open for me, and now it was a regular part of my day. It was amazing to me how many different mechanical methods there are for allowing boats to pass under or through bridges. By 7:30 we were in Little River, South Carolina, finally back to my home state. It had something of a quaint appealing look, with shrimp trawlers and waterfront restaurants, but it also had three casino boats and lots of condos. The marina at Crickett Cove looked nice, with an upper deck restaurant overlooking the boat basin.

We saw lots of boats, marinas and condos as we approached

Keeping Us Afloat

North Myrtle Beach, including Barefoot Landing, an outlet mall on the waterway with free docking for transient boats. We also passed LOTS of golf courses, a Myrtle Beach favorite. One of the courses included a cable car that went over the waterway to take the golfers from the parking area to the course. Worn out from the long days driving the boat, at 9:30 a.m. I went below to take a 20 minute nap that stretched into an hour.

After waking, I piloted us through the Waccamaw River while Capt. Rick napped. The river is a study in contrast, with rotting remains of seawalls from rice plantations gone for over a hundred years facing luxury homes with new seawalls and docks. At 2 p.m. we left the Waccamaw and entered Winyah Bay, where we steamed past Georgetown. Along the way we'd been chatting on the radio with Sea Dream, a classic Trumpy yacht that had been docked next to us in Norfolk. Sea Dream was designed and built by John Trumpy & Sons in Annapolis in 1966 for John M.L. Rutherford of Sands Point, NY, and Palm Beach, FL. Mr. Rutherford and his wife were famous powerboat racers, and "Sea Dream VII" was his third Trumpy yacht. She joined more than 200 custom Trumpy yachts built for the 20th Century's "Rich & Famous", like James Deering (International Harvester), Francis DuPont, Roger Firestone, and John Kimberly (Kimberly-Clark). The most famous Trumpy yacht is the "Sequoia", the Presidential Yacht from 1932 until 1977, serving nine Chief Executives, including John F. Kennedy. Trumpy Yachts epitomize the "Golden Era of Yachting", and they hold a revered place in

American Maritime history. This classic Trumpy was built of mahogany, with a square sided deck cabin and a smokestack on the roof that looked like it belonged on an Italian cruise liner. Very 1960's.

The current owner had run part of the way outside in the Atlantic, but had come back to the ICW because of the high waves. He was surprised to see us ahead of him with his faster boat. He passed us, but not for long. A couple of hours later we saw him anchored at sunset in the sawgrass outside of Estherville in the Minim Creek Canal. We thought he was ready for cocktail hour, but when we called him on the radio it tuned out that he'd broken a clutch cable, leaving him unable to take one engine out of gear. By the time they got the engine stopped, they'd run into a mud bank. He was working on it, but said they could get to Florida on one engine if necessary, so we wished him luck and continued our trip. I shot a nice picture of a shrimper returning to McClellanville at sunset as we neared our destination. The navigating got tricky after dark, but with a half moon in the sky and by illuminating the markers with a spotlight, we were doing well and making good time.

Just as we were congratulating ourselves on a great job, our arrival in Charleston got a little too exciting in the dark. We came out of the canal off Harbor River through Sullivan's Island around 7:30 p.m., and entered Charleston Harbor, where we were faced with a confusing number of flashing lights, all at great distances.

The backlight from the city made it next to impossible to pick them out. We could find no markers where we expected them, and quickly ran aground. We were able to back off of the shallow spot, and we used the location of the bridges as landmarks, but the twin spans of the giant Cooper River bridge were mistaken as two separate bridges, and we ran aground three more times. At that point, we discovered we were near Shute's Folly Island, surrounded by shallow water. It was impossible to find markers, and every time we headed for one we ran into shallow water. Captain Rick was getting frustrated and angry.

We finally saw a barge tug headed for home, and followed him until we were back in a channel. I spotted the Ashley River Bridge, and from there it wasn't too difficult to locate the marina, although there still were very few channel markers. Nighttime navigating in the twisting channel had been a bigger challenge than we'd expected. We arrived at the City Marina gas dock at 10 p.m., tired and exasperated. I'd been looking forward to a great seafood dinner at the marina restaurant that I'd visited before, but the restaurants were all closed. We ate sandwiches from the convenience store, I finally got a shower, and then walked the docks to admire the yachts before heading to bed. We'd be getting up at dawn again after about five hours sleep. We'd traveled 88 miles that day, 531 for the trip. Our time was running short to be home by Thanksgiving.

In addition to wanting to make it home for the holiday meal, this was the longest I'd been away from my commercial photography business since I'd started it 14 years earlier, and I was worried about my absence. I'd left Jenny to watch things, but she wasn't too interested in the business in those days.

Our partnership had been different in the beginning. When I departed the newspaper business to start a commercial studio, Jenny had been supportive. She'd set up the book keeping, and given me help with suggesting clients to call on. It had been a slow start, but the arrangement for publications photography with Furman kept us afloat. I was working part time at two thirds of my newspaper salary with full benefits. I always called it the world's best part time job. The studio business was an expensive undertaking. I had to purchase lights, more camera gear, and a computer for billing and book keeping. The first year I spent more on equipment than we earned, keeping the bills paid with credit cards. Slowly, I started to get work. I was hired by a local bank to shoot promotional shots during the filming of a TV commercial. Then the TV production company liked my work, and hired me to shoot promotional stills of them at work filming two more series of spots for a local hospital. Then the ad agency for the hospital bought stills from the TV commercials for a print campaign.

By the second year I was busy and making money at last. But, big surprise, Jenny wasn't happy. I'd encouraged her to take shoots for commercial clients, but she didn't have the confidence. I offered to assist her and help with any technical challenges, but she said I made her too nervous. So I called on clients and she didn't, and I got all of the work. Jenny had named her pet photography business Willow Wind Images, and while that worked for her, no one I called on could remember it. They wanted to remember my name, not something fanciful. So I changed it to Crosby Images over Jenny's protests.

For the first couple of years, Jenny did the bookkeeping and worked as my assistant. Then, as my worked picked up, she complained that she was spending so much time helping me, that she didn't have time for her own work. To make her happy, I hired a part time assistant.

Soon, Jenny was complaining about feeling left out! There was just no pleasing her.

As my business grew, it also began to take over the house. We lived in a suburban home with high peaked ceilings, and soon those heights beckoned me to leave the eight foot ceilings of the basement behind. The problem was that the main floor also had hideous rust colored shag carpets, and I needed a hard surface to work on. There was nothing but particle board under the carpets, so I thought I'd just get a hardwood floor put in. When the quotes came back at over $2,000. for the one room, I knew I'd have to find another way. I started calling around, looking for used hardwood flooring salvaged from old buildings. I soon discovered that the problem was that the labor cost more than the flooring, so no one sold it. I finally found a one man salvage operation who had a contract to salvage a large stone house on the Bob Jones University campus that was about to be demolished. He was saving all that he could before the school tore it down, and he said he had four days left. He'd sell me the 80 year old oak flooring for $40. a room. The only catch was that I had to take it out myself.

No problem, how hard could THAT be? I showed up the next day with two hired helpers, each of us with hammers and crow bars. I slid the crowbar under the edge of the first piece, hammered it in under the board, and it broke. Hmmm, maybe I needed to be more gentle. I slid the crowbar under the edge, tapped a little, slid it halfway up tapped a little more, and it broke. I went into the other room and found the salvage expert to ask him what I was doing wrong. He laughed, and gave me a lesson.

"It's easy", he said. " You put the crowbar under the end of the board, and raise it a half inch. Then you move it six inches at a time down the board, until you have the whole board raised a half inch. Then you go back down the board six inches at a time, until you have the whole thing out."

"That will take forever, doing this one board at a time." I said

He laughed and said "That's why nobody salvages hardwood flooring!"

I was discouraged, but undeterred. My helpers and I spent two days pulling eight rooms of flooring loose, one small increment at a time. In the beginning we broke a few boards, but got better and better as the days wore on. We'd been told the house was scheduled for demolition Monday, and they wouldn't let us work on Sunday because of BJU's religious rules, so we had two days to work. We hauled the piles out into the yard, still full of nails, because the deadline wouldn't allow us to take the time for pulling them.

After two exhausting days, all the boards were out and piled. On Monday, I spent another day hauling them to my house, then the better part of a week pulling nails. My hands were full of cuts and splinters, but I had my flooring for $320. Naturally, after all of the rushing, BJU didn't get around to tearing the house down for another month.

The next chore was to sort the boards. When doing hardwood floor installation, the flooring is tongue and groove, with the tongue on one side of the board and the groove on the other. There are also tongue and grooves on each end of the board. Since my 80 year old boards had been previously installed, everywhere they came to an end at a wall, they had been cut off. That meant to avoid wasting anything, the boards had to be sorted into nine piles. Short, medium and long boards cut on the left end, short medium and long boards cut on the right, and short, medium and long boards intact on both ends. Putting the floor together was like a giant jigsaw puzzle, always searching for just the right sized piece to avoid cutting any length and wasting it.

The first step of the floor installation was to go to the local library and check out a Wally's Workshop video titled "Wally does floors". Next I rented a manual floor nailer, one where you load it with a slider full of cut nails, position it on the tongue of the board, take a 10 pound mallet and hit it once to set the nail, and another to drive it snugly into place. Four thousand cut nails and eight thousand swings of that ten pound mallet later, I had a beautiful floor. It took two solid weeks of work to install, but it was a work of art. I hired a company to sand and finish it, and it was ready for business.

After installing the flooring, the master bedroom became the studio office, the kitchen and breakfast area became the client lounge, and the master bath became the model's dressing room. It turned into a terrific studio, but our living quarters and private area became two small rooms off the balcony overlooking the studio.

Between shooting at Furman University and calling on clients as I struggled to build my advertising client list, I was staying pretty busy. Vacations were always trips to Florida to see Jenny's parents. My parents made the trip from Chicago several times a year to see us, but Jenny's folks felt we should do the traveling, not them. So when Furman's football team made a surprising run through the playoffs and got a berth in it's first ever national championship game in Tacoma, Washington, I leaped at the chance for travel. I'd never been out west before, and my parents had been married in Tacoma when my father was stationed there at the end of World War II, so I was eager to go.

After convincing my sports hating boss in Furman's Marketing Department to send me, I discovered that since Furman was chartering a large jet to send everyone, Jenny could go with me for just $200. What an opportunity! I called her with the exciting news and told her to start packing, as we'd be leaving the next morning. Her response was disappointing.

"Oh David, I just can't! I don't have anyone to watch the

dogs, I'd need to do laundry, there's just no way I can be ready that fast."

And so I spent five days in Tacoma and Seattle without my bride. It was to be just the first of a long string of travel disappointments with Jenny. Prying her out of the house and away from her pets got harder and harder over the ensuing years.

It turned out that Jenny was glad she didn't make the trip. My time in Tacoma was wonderful, but the flight was pretty hairy. We were flying in a charter ATA L-1011, a huge plane carrying around 350 passengers. The Furman football team, coaches, the university president and all of the executives, all of the state sports press corp and several photographers were on the plane, along with a fair number of fans. There was not a seat to spare. We took off as scheduled in the morning, and flew as far as Indianapolis before we were forced to land in a blizzard. Funny thing was that the blizzard wasn't the problem, it was the weather on the west coast. Seattle was socked in solid with fog, and nothing was taking off or landing. Being a charter, there was no gate space for us in Indianapolis, and we sat on the tarmac in the plane for five hours, sweltering without air conditioning as the blizzard raged outside our windows.

Finally late in the evening, we were cleared for take off, heading once again for the suburban Seattle-Tacoma Airport, known as SeaTac. As we neared the west coast, the ground below us disappeared in a sea of clouds, and we didn't see land for the last few hours of the flight. As we approached Seattle, we could see tall radio towers rising above the clouds, but no buildings. Then, the plane began to dive down into the fog, going down, down, until suddenly rising up again to continue circling. That was interesting, I thought. Now we were all a little nervous. The captain was silent, not telling us why we did the dive and climb maneuver. Then we dove into the fog again, down, down, down, until again we climbed back up above the fog.

Now we were really nervous, everyone on the plane wondering why the captain wasn't updating us on our situation. After a few more minutes of circling, we dove a third time into the fog, this time going down, down, down, down until we suddenly cleared the fog, and found ourselves in a neighborhood! We were screaming down a two lane street in our giant L-1011, and we could see the mannequins in the shop windows we were so low to the ground. Just as we braced for the crash we believed to be imminent, the plane cleared a low fence and glided to a landing. The entire group of passengers burst into spontaneous applause at our deliverance from certain death. It turned out that we had been diverted to Boeing Field, where they test Boeing's new planes, rather than landing at the suburban SeaTac airport. That's why the neighborhood had been so close to our landing zone. We were the only plane to land that night. The sports reporter in the seat next to me said he'd been flying to games for 30 years, and had never been that scared.

The week in Tacoma was wonderful, and I found the church where Mom and Dad had been married back in the 1940's. I also squeezed time in the schedule for a quick trip to Seattle, where I saw the Space Needle, just to say I'd been. The night of the championship football game came quickly, and in the first half it looked like Furman would run away with the title, going up by several touchdowns. The second half was a whole different ballgame. Georgia Southern stormed by Furman to take the lead, and the two teams traded scores after that, with Furman scoring the go ahead touchdown with just over a minute left on the clock. Once again, Georgia Southern raced down the field, scoring the winning touchdown for a 44-42 victory in the final seconds, winning the 1AA National Title. It was a depressed bunch of players and fans who sat in front of the hotel in buses, waiting for word that we were heading to the airport.

Our jet was parked at Boeing Field, and the weather was still foggy, with no planes taking off or landing. So we sat in the buses until 2:30 a.m. that morning, when we finally started the drive to the airfield. When our caravan of buses arrived, we saw a jumble of huge jets near the hangers, but ours was not among them. After conferring with the tower by walkie talkie, the buses headed for the loop road around the field, a sad convoy looking for a ride home. At the other side of the airfield we found our ATA jet, sitting tall and proud, lights on, engines warmed up and ready to go. The only problem was that there were no stairs leading to the two story tall plane. We sat there in the buses staring at it for a few minutes, until the engines started to whine as they spun up to speed, and the jet taxied away. The buses turned around, and our convoy returned to the loop road, all the way back to where we started. When we arrived back at the hangers, a staircase had been rolled against the plane, but there was no ground crew. Since this wasn't a commercial airport, that wasn't part of the service. So at about 3:30 a.m., the dejected football team got off the bus and loaded everyone's luggage into the hold of the plane. We boarded and the jet took off, making it's way back to Greenville. The cabin crew woke us up at 5 a.m. to serve dinner.

With this being a charter flight, there was little to no flight information available on the ground in Greenville, and when we arrived around six hours late, we were greeted with a lot of hysterical relatives, all of whom believed the plane must have crashed. It wasn't the best of trips, but I was still glad I'd gone. Jenny was glad she hadn't.

We lived that way for a couple of years, me working, Jenny spending less and less time in the office, and our relationship limping along. As the business continued to grow, we looked for a way to combine a more commercial space in downtown Greenville with living quarters. Greenville, like many downtown areas, had a lot of vacant buildings. When the retailers moved to the malls in the 70's, the restaurants fled with them, and Main Street dried up as a location for business. Now the mayor was pushing the idea of people living and working downtown, and we thought that sounded great.

I found a commercial realtor, and began the long process of looking at vacant buildings that were in our narrow price range.

We looked at many ratty, leaking buildings, several of which became Greenville landmarks over the later years. One of the first was the trolley barn, where the town's trolleys had been based. It was a massive brick building with a slate roof and copper gutters, and we could have bought it for $90,000. in the depressed downtown real estate market of the time. But with a hole in the roof and mostly dirt floors, we just wouldn't have had enough money for the renovation. Spaghetti Warehouse later bought the building, and was reported to have spent a million dollars on the upfit. It's now the home of an architectural firm and North Hampton Wines, a wine store and upscale restaurant.

Another prospect was a two story building on Washington Street just off of Main. It was attractive to us because being multi story, it would have been easier to have a residence upstairs. When we went in the cellar with the realtor, we discovered hundreds of pigeon skeletons littering the floor. We were pretty grossed out when we were told that the rats were eating the pigeons, leaving only the bones behind! The two upper floors were later renovated into Barley's Tap Room, and the cellar is now the trendy Trappe Door restaurant and pub. We ultimately passed on the building because the support poles would interfere with the need for an open shooting space.

The last building we looked at was the old synagogue on Townes Street, just a block off of North Main. I had been contacted about it a couple of times, but had passed on it, as I didn't want to be the "photographers in the old church." I really wanted something more like a warehouse, concrete floors and high ceilings. The catch was the high renovation cost of those spaces, especially for the living quarters. Finally, running out of options, I agreed to go look at the building. I went with Jenny and our assistant Marilyn, and on a cold January day we walked into the sanctuary of what was currently the Faith Tabernacle Apostolic Church. The church had been in the building for 10 years, and they were looking to move to a more convenient location in the suburbs.

The building had originally been Temple Beth Israel, Greenville's first synagogue, built in 1929. When I walked in and saw the 20 foot ceilings and hardwood floors, I was hooked. The only disappointment was the dome. From the outside the 12 sided dome on the roof of the building was a great feature, and I couldn't wait to see it from the inside. Upon entering the sanctuary though it was nowhere to be seen. The church had thought the flat ceiling and dome didn't look "churchy" enough, so they had installed a peaked ceiling of acoustical tile from front to back, and built it right over the dome. I borrowed their 17 foot step ladder, climbed to the top, and lifted a panel to get a peek at the dome. It was dusty and needed painting, but looked generally intact.

The lower level had been the Sunday School rooms, and with their 10 foot ceilings would make a wonderful apartment.

Best of all, the building was occupied and in pretty decent shape.

I thought we could make it into a dream studio and home with the limited amount of money we had in our budget. Now we just had to find the money for the purchase.

Chapter Thirteen
Friday, November 19th

Captain Rick and I were both exhausted from the late night arrival, and we were 7:30 a.m. leaving Charleston. We spotted the ICW channel pretty easily just across from the marina, but we were really watching the marks after last night's experience. We waited 20 minutes at the LimeHouse Bridge in Charleston where we talked on the radio with Mont & Cynthia McMillen aboard Cielito, their 1930 Stephens yacht. The boat was a beauty, fully restored and with powerful twin diesels, as fast as it was gorgeous. They were taking it from their home in Orinda, California, near San Francisco, through the US waterway system, down the ICW, through the Panama Canal and back to California. They were making quite a trip, and were posting a web site of their progress. We promised to send them some pictures of their boat, and we

Keeping Us Afloat

traveled together through the day, slowing pulling away from them as they puttered along at less than their top speed.

At 11:30 I had to tiptoe through the shallow waters around Edisto Island and under the Edisto Bridge, where I got badly waked by a sundeck cruiser, rattling Captain Rick as he tried to nap. As things crashed below decks from the rude boater's wake, Rick came charging up the ladder to find out what had happened. So much for that nap. The ICW goes around Edisto Island, so I didn't see the marina or many familiar sights although I had vacationed there often. We were passed by a big cruiser, "Whale", out of Northbrook, Illinois, a boat that we would later see tied up in Beaufort, SC. At 12:20 we entered the Ashepoo Coosaw Cutoff, and by 2:15 we were passing through Beaufort into Port Royal Sound. The old homes and classic buildings make a great scene with all of the boats in the harbor, definitely worth a return visit. By 5 p.m. we were passing Harbour Town on Hilton Head Island and it's familiar lighthouse on the Calibogue Sound. I'd been there many times for work and pleasure, including covering the Heritage Golf Tournament, with its 18th green finale in sight of the lighthouse.

As the sun set we turned into the channel rounding Daufuskie Island in sight of it's old wooden lighthouse. The lighthouse is the only thing I recognized from my first trip there some 17 years earlier, when it had a tiny population, no paved roads and access was difficult. Now there are luxury homes, a golf course, a marina and numerous boat shuttle services between the island and Hilton Head. I'm not sure if I'd consider that progress.

At 5:30 we entered the aptly named Dark Creek, for a scenic and uneventful trip until we approached the Savannah River ship channel at 6:30 p.m., after the sun had set. The ICW waterway crossing of the channel was confusing and poorly marked, and as we slowly made our way across, I noticed a large ship approaching in the distance. It closed on us with surprising speed, and we picked up the pace, scooting into the channel as it passed closer than I preferred behind us. At 7:30 that evening we approached the huge Palmer Johnson shipyard just past Savannah, where we tied up among the yachts at the gas dock. The dock front restaurant was still open, and after a nice dinner, we turned in early to catch up on lost sleep. We'd traveled 95 miles in a long day, 626 miles for the trip so far. We had less than a week to finish the trip, and we weren't quite halfway there.

During the day's conversations Captain Rick had been fascinated to hear that I owned a synagogue. When I'd first found the building and decided that it was the place for us, I'd been a little naive about what a challenge financing it would be. My plan was to sell our house and use it for the down payment. It would cover about half of the cost of the building, and we were only asking the bank for about $40,000. in renovation costs, a modest amount even in those days. I planned on making that enough by doing much of the work myself.

My photography business had been growing by leaps and

bounds, our credit was good, and I felt like it would be attractive to the local banks. Boy, was I wrong. First I went to American Federal, the bank where I had kept my account ever since moving to Greenville. They were also a regular client, and I had photographed their CEO many times. When I presented my proposal, accompanied by drawing and photos, along with the purchase and renovation plans, the loan officer was enthusiastic.

What a great building, what a great plan, the bank is excited to be a part of this! I went home thrilled to tell Jenny the good news. Imagine my disappointment when three days later the loan officer called me to say "We're going to have to pass."

I was unprepared for this, and asked him why.

"Well, you're self employed, you've only been in business three years, come see us when you have been profitable for five or six years.

I asked "OK, if I come back in two or three years for a loan on the same building, would you do it then?"

He hemmed and hawed before admitting the truth. "The folks upstairs don't see old church buildings as a good risk. They feel that they are too purpose built, not really suitable for other uses."

I pointed out that this was a two story rectangular building with high ceilings, no steeple, no stained glass, just a big rectangular building.

But he'd been given the decision from above, and there was no appealing it.

So I went to another bank, and they loved it. What a great building, what a great plan, etc. Then three days later, "We'll have to pass."

I went to the third bank, and made my pitch again. The young loan officer was just as enthusiastic as the first two.

"What a great building, what a great plan, we are excited about this!" When I called him three days later to check on the progress, I wasn't surprised when he said "We're going to have to pass."

But I was angry. A part of my personality has always been not to let others tell me I can't do something. Being told that a goal is forever beyond my reach just makes me more determined to show them how wrong they are.

So I told Jenny that night "This bank is going to give us a loan, or that loan officer and I will both die trying!" In retrospect, I should have gone to as many banks as it took to find one who believed in the project. I spent the next three months butting heads with the bank. Every time they came up with a reason it wouldn't work, I came up with an answer to solve the problem. My stubbornness got the project through, but it didn't do much for my working relationship with the bank.

Regardless, we were moving ahead with the renovation planning while the loan was being processed. I hired a noted architect in town who I was acquainted with to help design the studio and complete drawings for the building codes reviews. He loved the old synagogue, particularly the two huge palladium windows on the two sides of the building. At 12 feet wide and 12 feet tall at the peak, they dominated the room. Unfortunately, they would also provide a lot of uncontrolled light that I didn't want. I did the majority of my studio shoots using powerful strobe lighting, and having the studio awash with light from the windows would just make the work tougher. I told the architect that I would likely cover the windows, so not to worry about them.

I wanted the office on the left, and the darkrooms and bathroom on the right, with a center opening into the studio shooting space from the foyer. My concept for the interior was for the walls to recede from the center like the bellows of a view camera, so that they left a clear angle of view for shooting, much like an amphitheatre in reverse. But when the architect came back with his first drawings they were a surprise.

He had the office in the left, the darkroom in the middle where I wanted my entry to the studio from the foyer, and a high ceilinged employee break room on the right. On both sides, the soaring windows were the highlight. The only way into the main studio shooting space was through the office. I explained one more time to him what my goal was, and sent him back to the drawing board.

He soon returned with another set of sketches, which once again featured the soaring windows at the expense of everything else. Now it wasn't as if I'd said "Just be creative, let your ideas flow." I had shown him what I wanted, and where I wanted it and why. This time in frustration I showed him my sketch again, and said "I want walls there, there, there and there, can you draw that!?" This time he drew what I wanted. The top half of the palladium windows were featured on the balcony, but otherwise covered in the office and darkroom. (Windows in a darkroom are a problem for obvious reasons.) He was very unhappy over my design requirements, and he didn't enter the building again for over a decade. Ironically, the design was so distinctive and well conceived that he received compliments on it many times from those who had seen it. He reportedly snarled at the unwanted kudos.

Drawings and remodeling contracts in hand, I met with the city building and fire inspectors to do a walk through. The mayor had been pushing the idea of attracting people to live and work downtown, and the Main Street area was starting to see the development of apartments in the upper floors of the shops. Unfortunately, the building inspectors were not on the same page as the mayor. I met the inspectors in the parking lot of the temple, and walked toward the building with the fire marshal, telling him about my plans as the chief building inspector gathered his notes at the car. I told him "I'm building a photography studio upstairs, and plan to live downstairs."

The fire marshal stopped in his tracks, turned to me and repeated, "You want to build a photography studio upstairs and live downstairs?"

I said yes, and he turned to the Building inspector, who walked up to us from his car.

"Hey Dick", he said. "He plans to build a photography studio upstairs, and live downstairs."

The inspector turned to me and said "Son, you haven't bought this building yet, have you?"

That was the start of a long and painful relationship with the building and fire codes people in downtown Greenville. In spite of the mayor's drive for downtown living, the codes people treated commercial and residential space as completely separate areas, and they wanted a two hour fire separation between them. That means that theoretically a fire could rage out of control for two hours in one floor before it spreads to the other floors. Very difficult and expensive to achieve. But I was not easily deterred, and finally came up with a plan that was doable and satisfied the inspectors. It involved firewalls, metal fire doors and automatic closers, but it wouldn't break the bank.

My contract to purchase the building was good for 90 days, plenty of time to get the financing complete. The bank kept me jumping through hoops, and the fact that my loan had a guarantee from SBA, The Small Business Administration, made it even more complex. As the deadline approached, we had the closing set for the last day before the contract expired.

I called the banker and told him "I'm leaving town tomorrow for a three day shoot all across the state. The day I return is the day we close the sale on the synagogue. If there is anything else that needs to be completed before then now is the time to tell me." He assured me there were no more issues, and that if anything came up, he could handle it. I told him I'd see him at the closing on Friday, and we said our goodbyes.

My photo shoot was a fun one, traveling the state with my client Dave Koss from Liberty Life, shooting their agents in the field. We photographed them in offices, nursing homes, old shacks, shrimp boats, and even on a hog farm. That turned out to be the most eventful, when were ushered into the piglet nursery. It was kept 80 degrees and humid for the piglets, and the stench when we entered sent us running for the door and retching. The only way I could get photos was to take a deep breath, run in the door while holding it in, and shoot until I had to race outside to take another breath. When we went to lunch afterwards, we discovered that we were attracting unwanted attention, as our clothes retained the awful smell. We went to a nearby drugstore for deodorizers and plastic bags, and had to bag our clothes and shoes for cleaning when we returned home.

Turned out the hog farm wasn't the only think that stunk. This was before the days of cell phones, and when I called my wife Jenny from the hotel at the end of the second day, the news was not great.

When our realtor had called the bank that day to inquire about why they hadn't received the closing papers, he was told "We can't possibly close Friday. Too many things are still incomplete." Now this is the same banker who two days before had told me that the bank was ready, there was nothing left to do. Unable to reach me in the field, Jenny surprised me by tackling the problem herself.

She called the bank, and demanded to know what the problem was.

The loan officer cited unspecified "Things" that had to be done before they were ready to close.

She reminded him that our contract was expiring, and he actually said "Well, if you have to do a new contract, maybe it will cost a little more, but you'll still get the building."

I was stunned, and very angry when she told me she had also discovered that our reluctant architect was a major account holder at the bank.

I'm not by nature a conspiracy theorist, but this was certainly looking fishy. It seemed our own architect could be working against us. Jenny took the bull by the horns and called our attorney. She explained the situation to him, and he called the loan officer at the bank.

Our attorney told him "Either you close on Friday as promised, or the Crosby's will be suing the bank for breach of contract." The banker backed down, and promised to send the closing papers the next day.

I spent a nervous day of shooting Thursday, wondering if the bank would call it off again. When I got back to Greenville again that night, Jenny told me the good news. Our attorney had the closing papers and the check in hand. Exhausted after the trip, I still spent the night tossing and turning, anticipating the purchase of our dream studio the next morning, but worried about what else could go wrong.

We got to the closing the next day, and while the seller and our Realtor were there, there was no one from the bank.

Our attorney said that he'd "Never seen a worse set of closing papers." The banker had obviously not expected to close, and had thrown them together at the last minute. Many areas of the mortgage contract were simply left blank for us to fill in. The interest rate on the loan was even blank. I filled it in at the agreed upon rate.

We completed the closing, the pastor from Faith Tabernacle handed us the keys, and we headed to the building to celebrate. The first thing I did on entering was take an extension pole and knock out eight of the acoustic tile panels covering the dome, letting them crash to the floor. After ten years, the dome was open again. Jenny and I sat on the stage at the front, opened a bottle of champagne, and toasted our incredible new studio and home. Now it was time to get to work.

Chapter Fourteen

I was now the proud owner of a 6,000 square foot, 1929 era synagogue. The building was constructed like a fortress, with one and a half foot thick solid brick walls. It had a lot of history as the first synagogue in Greenville, and when congregation Beth Israel moved to a more suburban location in the late 50's, it housed a Methodist church for five years. From 1964 to 1977 it was owned by the Greenville Labor Temple Cooperative, a group of labor unions who banded together to share the space in staunchly anti-union Greenville. I later heard stories of bread lines outside the building during a strike.

Then Faith Tabernacle spent ten years at the old temple at 307 Townes St., and now it was ours. The church had put a sign listing the time of their services in a concrete pad on a small square of dirt next to the building, and I'd seen old photos of the building that showed a tree in that spot. My first project became to remove the sign and the concrete, and plant a crepe myrtle there. It was very therapeutic after the struggles with the bank, and I spent a morning pounding the concrete into small chunks with a sledge hammer, thinking of my loan officer the whole time.

The contractors I met with advised me that the cost of labor was more than the value of salvaging materials would be, and that the most cost effective way to do demolition was to rip it out, throw it away and start fresh. With my tiny budget, I decided to do the demolition and salvage myself.

I soon started my demolition project so that I could clear the space for the new construction to start. The first thing was to remove a lobby partition and ceiling on the main floor, to remove the stage at the altar, and to remove the nursery room, which oddly had a raised floor. As I started dismantling it, I found out why. The building has a transept roof, cross-peaked front to back and side to side, with walls rising above the four low corners. The original design had run gutters inside the two front corners, behind the facade so that they were not visible. Very decorative, but according to our roofing contractor, a terrible idea.

"You never want to route water into a building." he said. "Roof lines and gutters are to keep it out of the building. That way if you have a leak, it leaks out, not in."

And of course, that's what had happened. The hidden gutters had leaked, and though exterior gutters were added later, the damage was done. As I removed the floors and walls of the nursery, I discovered a boarded up closet. The door was hanging from framing which ended above the floor. The rest had rotted away. Inside the closet, the floor was gone, and you could see into the lower level. What a mess. On the shelf in the remains of the closet were several small rusty holiday menorahs, which had been gathering dust there since the Jewish congregation left 30 years earlier.

The funny thing was, the Apostolic church had built an entire room, floors with joists, walls and ceiling, to distribute the weight away from this one crumbling corner, and then boarded the closet up to hide the damage. After I ripped the room out, all it took was a couple of new floor joists and a plywood floor to repair it. They had spent quite a bit more to just hide it.

The next big challenge was the ceiling. At 20 feet tall, I planned on removing the peaked acoustical tile ceiling and restoring it to the original flat plaster ceiling. When I started removing the ceiling panels, I discovered numerous holes in the plaster, and lots of cracks in the rest of it. The only economical solution was to remove the ceiling grid, and re-hang it as a flat ceiling. This included removing 22 four foot long fluorescent fixtures. After several days of back breaking labor, the ceiling was bare and ready to start work. Of course, with the light fixtures all gone, there was no light in the building at night. Fortunately we started the work in the spring and worked through the summer, so there was plenty of daylight to work by. The synagogue had originally contained windows of ribbed and starred glass, much of which remained on the boarded up lower level windows, but upstairs in the sanctuary the Faith Tabernacle folks had replaced all of the glass with red plexiglass. The effect when walking into the building was startling, as every surface was bathed in an intense red light. One neighbor told us that when he'd passed by the church during nighttime services, that it "looked like Hell Fire and Damnation coming right out of the windows!" Our immediate solution was to keep the large windows open to bring in some light while we worked on the construction.

During the upstairs demolition, I had saved every 2x4, every sheet of plywood, every door, every ceiling panel, and every light fixture to use for the new construction. I had even filled a trash can with all of the nails we pulled, and sold it to a scrap metal recycler. Nothing was going to waste. As construction started on the office side of the main floor, I moved downstairs with my demolition. The old Sunday school rooms were a bigger challenge. To minimize new construction with our tight budget, we were removing walls to combine rooms, with almost no new walls required. The seven class rooms with their long narrow hallway between became three bedrooms, a great room, and only a short vestige of the hallway. The two small half baths became a full bath with a large Jacuzzi tub completely filling what had been the tiny men's room. All of the kitchen cabinets were pulled out and replaced, and new appliances were brought in and installed. The entry to the old boiler room became the laundry room.

The elderly steam heat system was replaced with a heat

pump. Getting rid of the pipes and boiler wasn't easy though. I received a quote from the HVAC company of $800. to remove the steel pipes that carried the steam throughout the lower level, and which had originally connected with a series of radiators. In the interest of cost savings, I spent $200. to buy a reciprocating saw with steel blades, and cut them up and hauled them off myself. It was backbreaking work, but after selling the scrap steel for $80., my total cost was $120. and I owned a new saw.

The boiler was another thing. The HVAC contractor quoted me $500. to remove it. It was the size of a small car, and he said they were typically built with a steel shell over a cast iron firebox. The plan was to cut around the circumference of the half inch steel shell, pull the sides apart and then break up the brittle cast iron firebox with sledgehammers into small enough pieces to haul off. Sounded like a good plan, and I gave the go ahead. The workers showed up early the next morning with their acetylene cutting torch, and set to work cutting the shell in half. It took about an hour to cut the thick steel, and when they were done, they wedged crowbars into the gap to pull it apart. Only problem was that it wouldn't budge. After cutting several exploratory holes over the next hour, they gave me the bad news. This boiler had a steel firebox inside its steel outer shell, and they were connected by 60 one inch thick rods. The only way to cut it up was to cut 60 circles in the half inch steel around each of the 60 rods. A half day project thus became a day and a half project, with the workers having to refill the acetylene tank halfway through. That boiler had apparently been designed to withstand a nuclear blast. To their credit though, the HVAC contractor, Carolina Heating and Air, stuck to their price quote.

There was also a heating oil tank in the ground outside that had fed the boiler, and environmental regulations required its removal. It was shallowly buried, and I dug around it to expose the sides. Carolina Heating then brought a massive crane whose boom snaked down the narrow 15 foot space between the synagogue and the old wooden grocery building next door to snatch it out of the ground. The suction was so great that it took some effort, but the last piece of the old steam heat system was finally gone.

Construction was moving right along upstairs, but there were still surprises. I had somehow assumed that the fairly affordable quote to re-hang the ceiling, which had already been an addition to the budget, include replacing the 22 fluorescent lights. But no, as the ceiling went into place, I was told that it was a job for the electricians. Hanging the ceiling itself became an adventure. I didn't want to lose any of my 20 foot ceiling height, and asked that the ceiling be hung as high as possible. The contractor told me that at least eight inches of clearance was needed to be able to slide the light fixtures into the grid at an angle, lift them above the grid and drop them back into place. So eight inches it was. There was only one problem. The ceiling grid installation was done with a laser installed in one corner, and the installers used a mirror at each location where they set another grid hanger to keep it at the same level. As they approached the dome, they noticed the hangers were getting shorter and shorter. After discussing it with the contractor, he came to me with the problem.

As he explained "The transept roof structure all ties together in the center. Except in the center of this roof, the middle is a hole where the dome is, and the weight of the dome over time has caused the ceiling to sag four inches."

I was worried, and asked if this was an unsafe structural problem.

He laughed and said "The support structure around that dome is incredible, and it's all built from heart pine. You have to drill holes to drive a nail, because it's as hard as steel. If I'd built this and it had sagged that small amount in 60 years, I'd be thrilled."

So the ceiling work continued, and I met with the chief electrician about the cost of reinstalling the lights. Hanging the ceiling had cost $1200., and I was stunned when he told me that the cost of hanging and wiring the 22 fixtures was $100. per light, or $2,200. total. I told him we just didn't have that much money, and he said that amount was $50. to hang them, and $50. to wire them in flexible steel conduit. If I wanted to hang them myself, I could cut the cost in half. When I'd planned this renovation, the money we'd borrowed from the bank was all we had to do the project. Everyone, bankers, contractors, subcontractors, seemed to accept that there are always cost overruns, and that we would just find more money somehow.

I told them that we didn't have that option. I kept a written list, with a running total of the items to be completed, the estimated cost, and the total money remaining. Every time an item went over budget, another item came off the list of things to be done. It had to balance.

So, with a day worker helping, I stood on a 16 foot scaffold for two days, working the 25 pound light fixtures over my shoulders into the grid. In the areas closest to the dome, where we only had four inches of clearance, I had to take a hatchet and chop holes in the plaster ceiling above the grid to make room as I struggled to wedge the lights into place. It was finally complete, and as the lights were wired into place and turned on, we celebrated having lighting in the new studio. And at only double the original budget. Really more, because re-hanging the ceiling had not been part of the original plan.

The renovation contractor was a wonderful guy with the best intentions, but very inexperienced. His father was a noted area homebuilder in the luxury market, and Carl had started out as an electrician, moving into doing renovation projects as a contractor. When he'd first looked at my renovation plans, I'd made a list of all of the things I'd like to accomplish, and told him how much I had to spend. He walked through the old temple, looking at everything I pointed out, making notes as we went. One stop was under the front steps, in a vaulted area with iron barred doors that looked like they belonged in a jail cell. The church had built a makeshift baptismal pool down there from concrete blocks, and the contractor was curious about the uncapped 220 volt outlet just above the surface of the water. Carl asked it's purpose, and I explained that the church filled the pool with a garden hose, and then put a water heater element in to heat it, plugged into the 220 outlet.

He was appalled at the thought of the 220 outlet being inches above the water as people splashed about in the baptismal pool, and quipped "What a concept. You save em, and then you fry em!"

Carl continued to walk through the building, checking items on my list. I thought he might be able to do as little as half of my wish list within my budget, and when I asked him how much of it he thought he could do, I was amazed.

"All of it" was his reply.

"Wow, that's great! How long do think it will take?" I asked."

"Oh, I think three weeks, but lets say a month to be on the safe side."

I was ecstatic, but should have remembered the old words of wisdom. Anything that seems too good to be true, probably is.

We were now in the fourth month of construction, and not done yet. I was anxious to move in, and was doing much of the finish work myself, including putting over 60 gallons of paint on the newly restored walls. All while keeping the photography business running so that the cash continued to flow. I was doing everything but sleeping.

One afternoon Carl came to me, very agitated. He was hopping from foot to foot, like a little kid who had to pee.

"David", he said, "We've got a big problem". Seems that while Carl had worked with a budget and contract on the main floor electrical work, he had considered the lower level, with few new walls, to be a minor project. As a former electrician, he had planned on doing the work himself to save money. Now his contracting work kept him busy on other projects as he struggled to maintain cash flow, so he had told the electricians to "Just go ahead and do the lower floor too." No budget, no limits.

Now even a construction novice like me knew you never give anyone a blank check, especially in the construction industry. A light fixture installation that is budgeted for $50. under contract, might cost triple that when you're paying on a time and materials basis. One guy installs the fixture, another holds the ladder, another fetches parts, and costs skyrocket because of the lack of a budget. The chief electrician had met with Carl that day, and told him that their costs were at $3,500., an amount more than the total costs of the upstairs electrical work. The budget had been $1,500. downstairs, and $3,000. upstairs. And that didn't count the extra $1,100. I'd paid to wire the 22 fixtures into the studio ceiling. Carl's decision to turn the electricians loose downstairs had created a huge budget shortfall, and we were still at least a month from completion of the project. I didn't know where the money would come from, but told the contractor that I'd try to find it somewhere.

Meanwhile, the renovation dragged on. The list of

unfinished items for which there was no money was growing. The balcony received its required steel guardrails, fashioned for a low budget by an older black man known locally as "Iron Man". His normal work was replacing the picketed vertical porch rails on small urban houses, but when I showed him my design of horizontal pipes for the top and middle rails, with smaller pieces in between for decorative effect, he was intrigued and said he could do it. He pre welded all of the L shaped sections after measuring just one of the corners, and was dismayed when he discovered that there were slight variations in each section of the balcony. It wasn't drawn that way on the blueprints, but with our low budget workers, it was no surprise. He spent the better part of a day cutting the sections apart and re-welding them to fit, while I raced around laying plywood sheets to keep the sparks from the welding from landing on my newly refinished hardwood floors. The plywood floored balcony would remain bare until months later, when increased business would provide money for carpeting.

During the hot summer of working on the new studio I also had to make time to take on photo shoots to support the business and keep the bills paid. I had photographed Freedom Weekend Aloft, a regional hot air balloon festival, several times over the past years, and was scheduled to shoot it again over the fourth of July holiday. This one turned out to have an unexpected twist. The festival had hosted as many as 200 balloons from across the country, and one of the highlights was the mass ascension, where all of the balloons took to the sky in the calm just before sunset.

Balloons need low winds to safely take off, and the mass ascensions have been postponed many times because the winds were too strong. This time, as more than 100 balloons took to the air as close to simultaneously as possible, the wind died completely. Not a breath of a breeze. I was aboard a balloon taking photos, and we all just hung there in the still air. Normally, as the balloons gain altitude they quickly drift apart in a light breeze, but not today. Balloons were all around us, above us and underneath us. We were leaning out of the basket and shoving other balloons away from us to keep from collapsing them or tangling lines with us. If a balloon were to come up underneath us, we could punch in its crown, causing a fatal crash.

The other problem was that the light breezes usually carried the colorful balloons far enough away from the launch site that the pilots could find a safe, open place to land, away from homes and power lines. This time, as all of the balloons hung together in a giant ball of color, we were barely drifting, and now the sun was starting to set. It's suicidal to land at night, because the chances of hitting power lines becomes very high in the low visibility. The mass of balloons had drifted over an older neighborhood, with large trees, power lines and fences everywhere, and as the darkness approached, the pilots were out of options. Our pilot landed in the small backyard of a house, the crew and I snatched the deflated balloon out of the way, and another landed where we had just been. That one was quickly removed as well, and a third balloon landed in the same spot as a fourth balloon landed on the street in front of the tiny house. There were balloons everywhere in that neighborhood, and it's fortunate no one was injured. The upside was that the festivals theme of "Paint the Sky" had truly been on display as the balloons all hung in one spot, and I'd gotten terrific photos of the panorama of color in front of me. I'd sell those balloon photos for years to come.

Back at the studio, I had told the builder I planned on moving in on August first, but they were nowhere near being finished. Two weeks later, I told them "That's it, I'm moving in!" Jenny declined to join me, remaining in our suburban home, keeping it for sale while I moved into the construction zone on the lower level. I figured my presence would pressure the workers to get finished and get out, but they seemed unperturbed. I slept in the front corner bedroom, which had no work going on in it, with a note on the door saying "Person sleeping, Do Not Disturb". Around 8 a.m. every morning, the hammering would start.

I'd stagger sleepily out into the hall in my bathrobe, past the electricians on ladders wiring ceiling lights who greeted me with "Mornin David." as I headed for the coffee pot. This went on a couple of more weeks, until in early September, I finally ordered everyone out. There was no more money and not everything was done, but I couldn't take it anymore. The cigarette butts ground into the floor, the nails lying in the bottom of our Jacuzzi tub, the coke bottles everywhere with chewing tobacco spit in them. They just had to go.

The day after the last worker packed his tools and left, the chief electrician met the contractor, Carl and me in the studio. "Well David, it was a tough one, but we got it done. Here's the bill." And with that he handed me a bill for $7,000.! Turns out when they'd given Carl the $3,500. figure, that was only for the work to that point. They'd worked for three more weeks after that. I was shocked, and asked how that was possible, being almost five times the original budget.

"You know, there was a lot more work to do than we thought, and time and materials does run a little higher." I told him "This is awful", and turned and handed the bill to Carl, adding "But Carl's the one who gets the bill. I pay him, and he pays you. He's the one who hired you."

The electrician sputtered his objections at this, knowing Carl had spent every nickel we'd paid him already, and said "Here's what I can do. If you sign this agreement to pay the $7,000. with interest over time, I'll work with you. Otherwise, I'll be forced to put a mechanic's lien on the building."

That would be a disaster, as the loan with the bank would be placed in technical default by having a mechanic's lien on the property. I told him I'd have to think it over, and he gave me three days to give an answer, or face the lien.

I contacted my attorney, who told me "I think you're stuck, but this isn't really my field. Let me recommend a construction attorney." My Dad was visiting from Chicago, and he and I made the pilgrimage to Sandy Stern's office high in a downtown office tower.

Sandy heard our story, and said "I don't think you owe him a dime. Hold on, let me check the statute." He went to retrieve a law book from the library, and returned to point to the open page triumphantly. "Just like I thought. You hired the contractor, and he hired the electrician. You've paid what you agreed to the contractor, and any side deals he made with the electrician are his responsibility, not yours. You tell him that if he puts a mechanic's lien on that building, you'll have the court remove it in about 30 minutes, and he'll be stuck with the legal fees."

We were ecstatic, and Dad and I drove back to the studio for our meeting with the electrician.

When he showed up, he said "OK David, what's it going to be. Will you sign, or do I put a lien on the building?" I told him "after consulting an attorney, here's the law. I hired the contractor, not you. He has been paid the amount we agreed upon. Any arrangement to the contrary is between him and you. If you put a lien on the building, we'll get it removed immediately and you will owe the legal fees." His reply was not what I expected .

He simply said "Oh well, it was worth a shot." He knew he didn't have a leg to stand on, he was bluffing.

The irony is that when the amount was $3,500. I was trying to figure out someway to pay it. When it hit $7,000., I had no choice but to call an attorney. If the electrician had been just a little less greedy, he'd have gotten paid.

The last hurdle was the final building inspection, required to receive our occupancy permit. Dick, the chief building inspector who'd been so skeptical of my plans arrived to do the inspection. I naively thought he'd walk through, say "Great job", pat me on the back and hand us the occupancy permit. After all, every step of the process had been approved, with inspectors checking walls, plumbing and wiring, all before we were allowed to move forward. But I was in for another surprise.

Dick walked through the building, shaking his head as made notes on his check list. "Looks like you've got a lot of work to do", he said. The inspector came up with a list of $10,000. worth of changes he wanted us to make to get an occupancy permit. Some were realistic. He said the firewalls in the stair well didn't meet the two hour fire rating, and would have to be made thicker. The metal doors didn't have automatic closers, and they would have to be added. Some of his demands were absurd. He wanted an awning built to cover the entire front of the building's wide stairs, giving it "covered egress." He didn't care that it would cost a fortune and ruin the look of the historic building. He wanted the fire escape railing made an inch taller, and an awning over its length. And the list went on and on. There was just no way to do all of this. We were out of money.

So I went to the codes office, and paid $75. from my dwindling funds for a copy of Southern Building Codes, the book used by the inspectors office. I spent hours pouring through the related statutes, finding loopholes and rebuttal arguments for nearly every request Dick the inspector had made.

When we met at his office, I read him chapter and verse for every code that we disagreed on. We mainly just had to fix the firewalls and closers in the stairwell, and the occupancy permit was ours.

We could legally move into our synagogue.

Chapter Fifteen
Saturday, November 20th

Up early again, Captain Rick and I left the Palmer Johnson shipyard in Savannah aboard the 'Waxing Gibbous' before dawn with a free newspaper and a dozen donuts compliments of the dockmaster. We passed a lot of gorgeous waterfront homes on Skidaway Island, then at 7:20 a.m. passed the Isle of Hope. It has a nice marina with a number of quaint homes in the background. Through the Skidaway Narrows, past Moon River, we were into the Vernon River by 8 a.m. This stretch of the ICW through Georgia is a torture chamber of twists and turns, followed by more twists and turns. Rick and I had to keep a close watch on the channel markers to avoid another grounding. At 1:30 we passed Wolf Island, a wildlife preserve, and we could see the Sapelo Island lighthouse in the distance.

Keeping Us Afloat

At 2 p.m. we passed Broughton Island thru Buttermilk Sound and made our way to Golden Isles Marina at St. Simon's Island to buy a set of Florida charts and to top off the fuel along with re-provisioning for the long night run. We had called ahead for the charts and had been told there was a courtesy car we could use to go for groceries. When we got to the marina at 4 p.m., we were told the car was reserved for overnight dockers, and that it was already out anyway. I went to the marina store for the charts, and tried without luck to find a ride. I did find a cab company, and paid them to pick me up, wait while I shopped at the Winn Dixie, and take me back.

Even though I ran through the store, it was after 5 by the time I got back. I told the driver the captain might keelhaul me, since we were trying to get through the St. Simon's ship channel and back into the ICW before dark. Sure enough, Capt. Rick was waiting impatiently at the marina driveway when I got back, and we threw all the groceries onboard, tossed the lines and took off into the sunset. We did make the channel before dark, but just barely. Rick wasn't too mad, and was really pleased when I told him I'd gotten everything on the list, including the sardines he had a craving for. We'd been told the run to Fernandina Beach was 40 miles, and with our 8.5 knot speed and a few no wake zones, we planned on a 5 hour run, putting us at the dock by 10 or 10:30 p.m.

We're still not sure what happened, but we turned the page on the chart and it said Fernandina Beach when we checked at 9 p.m. We arrived at the marina at 9:30, not even slowed by a near grounding outside of town, when we got the cross channel markers confused with a rangefinder. When you have five red lights flashing at you in the dark, it can get hard to find the right one. The sight on our approach wasn't what we expected for a town with a beach name, as we drove through a scene out of industrial hell, with belching smokestacks, thumping machinery and giant ship loading cranes with four legs that had the look of monsters ready to reach down and grab our little boat.

At the dock we got help with the lines from a man with diamond rings and a cigar, smelling of whiskey. He turned out to be the owner of "Good Time Charlie" a huge Viking Yacht Fisherman that had waked us earlier in the day. He had gotten quite a few complaints over the radio, as he politely called sailboats for permission to pass, and then did so at a speed which caused a huge wake, slamming the boats and throwing the contents to the decks. It was easy to see how he got the name for his boat.

We then ran to the dockside restaurant, which had quit serving. They sent us to a restaurant a few blocks away, which had also quit serving. Three or four more blocks, and we finally found an Italian place that served us in the bar. We watched the Holyfield-Lewis boxing match, which was taped from a week earlier. It was still new to us, since we hadn't seen much TV, heard a radio or read the news for 10 days. (Lewis Won.) We'd made an incredible 133 miles that day, something I still can't figure out. We were at 759 miles on the trip. I turned in at 11:30, resting for another early morning.

The twisting channels of the Georgia ICW hadn't kept us too busy to talk, and Captain Rick had been amused by all of the trials and tribulations of my renovation project. I told him how Jenny and I had moved into the residence downstairs at the synagogue, cleaning construction debris as we went. Many things were unfinished, primarily the asbestos tile floors which did not receive carpet for five more years. Six boarded up windows in our downstairs apartment waited two years to be replaced with Pella thermopane windows.

The studio was similarly unfinished, with carpet yet to come in the lobby, office, models dressing room and balcony. The planned studio kitchen was currently nothing but pipes hanging out of the walls. But we did have the regulation height basketball goal in the studio for afternoon relaxation, shooting hoops with a beer. It was fine playing upstairs on the hardwood floors, but to anyone in the lower level it sounded like a herd of elephants stampeding.

Most of the unfinished studio projects would get done in the next 12 months as business increased, and cash flow with it. One of the ironies was the reactions from clients.

"Wow, awesome new studio! We have a shoot for you, on location."

Business soared, partly because of the new studio and the image boost that went with it, but we weren't shooting in our new space. Everything was on location. For the first six months after occupying our domed studio, I did not do a single shoot in it. But I wasn't complaining. Business was business, no matter where it was, and I spent my evenings working on unfinished projects in the building.

One big problem was that our house where we lived before the synagogue still hadn't sold. It was in a borderline neighborhood on the edge of town, and sales in the area were slow. I finally sold it to a young couple and took back a second mortgage on it after holding onto it for a year, and within another year they had split up and defaulted. I was forced to take the house back, and a few months later sold it to a man who was waiting for what his lawyer described to me as a "Substantial financial award" on a workers comp claim for a back injury. The only catch was that he wanted to lease the house while he awaited his settlement check, which his attorney told me "Should be received in two weeks" The bank was pressing me to come up with the money from the sale towards my new studio, so I reluctantly took the deal.

The "Two weeks" turned into six months, and the new tenant's previously helpful lawyer hung up on me when I called and asked him about the delay. The tenant also called me one day to ask about cutting down "one or two" trees in the front yard. The 3/4 acre lot was covered in trees, many of them hardwoods, but the towering pines near the house were making him nervous. He'd had a tree fall on his house before, and didn't like the risk. I told him he'd have to wait until the closing, when the house would be his. When we finally closed a few months later, he startled me when just prior to the closing, he approached me in the closing attorney's lobby.

"You know those trees?" he said. "I cut them all down!"

I just about choked, but didn't say anything, ready to strangle him if this closing didn't go through. It went without a hitch, and afterwards I drove by the house for a look. The new owner had cut over 100 trees from the lot, many of them huge hardwoods. He had stripped it bare, and it looked horrible. I was glad the house was no longer my problem.

My commercial photography business had started in Greenville at a time when the advertising market was growing rapidly. Henderson Advertising was the behemoth of the local agencies, having won the National Ad Agency of the Year award in 1980. They had national and international clients, and I was not yet on their radar screen. But Henderson and smaller but very successful Leslie Advertising recruited talent from across the country, and when the revolving door of the ad business left them unemployed, many had fallen in love with the laid back pace and rolling foothills of Greenville, South Carolina. Their solution was to start their own ad agencies, which gave Greenville a robust advertising business much greater than the population would normally support. And so the Greenville agencies' talent pool grew, as they did projects for companies far from their southern base.

Breaking into working for the ad agencies had been my goal from the beginning. I didn't just want to make a living, I wanted to do the best work. I wanted to see my photography on billboards, newspaper ads, annual reports and brochures. I wanted to travel, and to do amazing imagery. But it was a slow process.

Doing photography for an ad agency is a different beast. I remember vividly one early sales call. It was to an art director I had previously been acquainted with at the Greenville News, who was now working with a local agency. His response to my little box of prints was very encouraging. "Very nice, you do great work" he said to me. "We'll definitely keep you in mind for future work." I went home thrilled, and awaited his call. When six weeks later, the phone had not rung, I called the art director back to see if any work was headed my way. "Have we met before?" was the answer.

At first I was offended that he could go from enthusiastic about my work to not even remembering my name. As I learned more about the pressures of the ad business though, I came to understand it over time. Art directors are constantly being called on by photographers from across the country, even in Greenville. Being a local source doesn't mean much to them, in part because, to paraphrase the bible, a photographer is not respected in his own home town. (I often joked that I should get a New York post office box.)

Advertising agencies have a constant pressure to produce. You are only as good as your last project, and if you screw up, you can lose the client. With a lost client comes a drop in income for the business, and staff gets laid off. You can literally lose your job if you hire the wrong photographer, one who doesn't deliver the promised work, or who causes a problem with the client.

It makes most art directors wary of hiring unknown talent. I found out the hard way that you have to constantly keep your work in front of them, until they eventually hire you for something small because their regular source is busy on another shoot. And if you do a great job, on time, on budget and with a smile, then the next time you get a bigger job. Their confidence in you grows, until you are their first phone call, and now you have a client. It takes time, patience, and a thick skin to deal with all of the rejection.

Typical of this was my experience with The Eison Goot Group, now known as Brains on Fire. They were a growing Greenville based agency when I went to call on them. I showed my little box of prints to Robbin, the art director, and she was completely unimpressed. Although she was polite and left it unsaid, "Don't call us, we'll call you" was the vibe I picked up. Then one of their clients, American Federal Bank, (now a part of SunTrust) hired me to do PR photography of a television commercial shoot for the bank. I spent a day following the film crew as they shot the commercial, images the bank would use for their newsletter.

The director of the film production company loved the idea of the 'behind the scenes' shots of his crew at work, and months later hired me to do PR shots for their use. I was to spend two very long days shooting behind the scenes images for Saint Francis Hospital, another Eison Goot client, and for Peeler's Dairy. The Saint Francis commercials were brilliant, with great visuals which I captured in addition to the shots of the crew at work. The theme was "Why you don't want a semi private room", and in one segment, the curtains slid back between the beds to reveal a loud guy smoking a cigar, then a kid jumping up and down on his father's bed shooting a toy ray gun, and finally a biker gang gathered around the bed of a fallen gang member, staring into the camera as a biker chick cleans her nails with a switchblade.

It was fun stuff, and the director was making sure I got it all.

The crew would finish the take, call 'Cut!', and roll the camera dolly back out of the way as they said "Ready for stills!"

That was me, and I'd step into the frame, taking 30 seconds to capture the same image on B&W film that the crew had just spent hours setting up. The cost of film production for TV is so high between the large crew and the expensive rented lighting, grip and camera gear that every minute counts. And I made my 30 seconds count as well. My newspaper experience had taught me to work fast and in low light, so I always got the shot.

After the shoot was over, the art director from Eison Goot called me to buy usage of the scene prints for newspaper ads. Since I'd been hired by the production company and not by the ad agency, they were mine to sell. And now I had my first substantial ad agency client.

It was providential that the first big intro into the agency world was for a hospital. I continued to do work through Eison Goot for Saint Francis Hospital, and then received a call from the art director at DeMint Marketing who hadn't remembered meeting me. (Yes, it's the company that was owned and run by later US Senator Jim DeMint.) The AD had seen my work for Saint Francis and wanted me to do a shoot for the Greenville Hospital System. Now I had two hospitals on my client list. The two agencies did a lot of work for their local hospitals, and because of that experience they soon picked up two more hospital clients each. And they hired me to shoot for them, so I now had six hospitals. Soon I became "That guy who shoots hospitals", and was shooting for hospitals across the Southeast because of my experience.

Hospitals are funny places. Because doctors are in the business of saving and improving lives, they can sometimes have rather large egos. They also don't have a lot of patience for marketing projects, or really for anything that doesn't directly involve their mission. To combine that with photographers, who are often known for having healthy egos themselves, can be a volatile mix. It's strange that when I was in the newspaper business, I considered my work as my own, and didn't really care too much if I pleased my employers or not.

In my commercial photography however, I wanted happy customers. And in my medical work, I always went into a project with the approach that "We are not the most important thing going on here." I learned to work with doctors and medical staff to adjust to their schedules and interruptions, and to put them at ease with respect and flexibility. Being allowed to photograph surgeries, ER scenes of life and death, hospice patients and children with cancer brings with it the responsibility of compassion and sensitivity. Having those traits meant they were always happy to have me back.

When I started traveling to hospitals, my wife Jenny usually went with me. My first assistant Marilyn only worked part time, and as an older lady, she wasn't too keen on overnight trips. Jenny usually got along well with the clients and hospital staffs, and having a woman along helped with the patients. I've often been told that I'm a "non threatening male", someone who, being soft spoken and even tempered, doesn't come across aggressively. I was not sure initially if that was a compliment or not, but I've grown to be happy with that perception, and it's served me well photographing at hospitals and medical facilities.

One of the first surgeries I photographed was for a hospital in Aiken, SC. The procedure was a lung lobectomy, where a lobe of the lung was removed on a Tuberculosis patient. I was scrubbed, gowned and masked, and stood just behind the surgeon as he made a long incision down the chest, blood welling up and being suctioned away. Then I watched, startled, as the doctor chiseled through the breastbone with a large silver chisel and mallet, the unconscious patient bouncing on the table with every strike of the mallet. When the surgeon inserted the spreader to spread the ribs apart, I went out into the hall to get more film from Jenny, who was assisting on the shoot.

When she saw me she asked "Are you OK? You look green."

I answered "They're cauterizing blood vessels", which is pretty much taking a soldering iron and burning off the small bleeders in the incision.

"Ooooooo, that even gets the nurses sometimes." said a passing nurse, and I could see why.

The smell of burning meat had me queasy, but I went back in with a fresh roll of film loaded. I watched as the liver and other organs were removed and set aside from the open chest cavity, still connected and functioning, but removed to allow access to the lung on the bottom. I stepped closer, and could see the pumping of the patients beating heart, amazed to share the privilege of watching this brutal but ultimately healing process of surgery. I spent an hour and a half shooting, and kept racing in to the hall saying "More film! more film!" as I burned through frame after frame of the medical drama in front of me. I have always enjoyed shooting surgeries, but there were none more exciting than this first major operation.

Another growth area for my business was aerial photography. I'd been hired a couple of times to do aerials of the city from helicopters, and this led to a 14 month contract to document the construction of Michelin's new North American Headquarters building in Greenville. Dubbed the "Crystal Palace" for its glass enclosed peaked atrium, I would document the work on the ground, and once a month rent a helicopter for aerials of the construction progress. Flying every month gave me the opportunity to keep updated aerials of the city, and I often piggy backed other clients aerials onto my trips. At $500. an hour for the small Bell Helicopter, it was very cost effective to make detours on an existing trip rather than charter the flight separately from the heliport on the fringes of town.

As my business grew, my clients were growing with me. When I'd called on Joe Erwin at Erwin-Penland Advertising in 1986, the agency consisted of Joe, his wife Gretchen, and a secretary. Joe had been encouraging, but confessed to me that he didn't really have any photography work yet. A Greenville native, Joe had started his advertising career at Leslie Advertising before heading off to the big time working for a New York City agency. Now he was back in Greenville, starting his own business. He was interested in having me photograph his grand opening reception, but really couldn't afford to pay my rates for the two hour long party.

I suggested a compromise.

"Tell you what Joe, I'll shoot half the time, and mingle the other half. You pay me for one hour, and I'll spend the rest meeting people." Joe thought that sounded great, and promised to send me some work when he finally had some.

The party was great, and I met a large number of Greenville advertising luminaries during the evening. Joe managed to get a cover shot and two page spread in Ad Week for his opening, and it was a success for both of us. It was another year before Joe had work for me again, but Erwin-Penland grew over time to be one of the largest agencies in the Southeast, with hundreds of employees, and became a major client for me. Their account MetroMobile was a pioneer in the local cell phone market, and EP was a regular sight in my new synagogue studio, shooting first bag phones, then clunky walkie talkie style "portable" phones, and finally much smaller cell phones. Through growth and corporate buyouts, MetroMobile morphed into a part of Verizon, and EP's share of their work has continued to grow over the years.

As much as Jenny wanted my success to continue, she was also jealous of it.

At one point shortly after we moved into the new studio, she confronted me, saying "This isn't even my business any more. You've completely taken over. All I do is assist and do the book keeping, while you do all of the shooting, and get all the glory. This is not fair!" I was surprised by her outburst, but was ready to accommodate anything she wanted.

"Tell you what", I said. "We'll split up the business. You do your pet photography, and I'll do the commercial work. I'll hire an assistant full time to take your place, and you can go back to being Willow Wind Images. You'll be completely separate. It will be your own business again." The problem with Jenny was that complaining was easier than working, and her lack of self confidence kicked in.

"Well, I'm not sure I really want to do that", she said quietly.

"What do you want to do then?" I asked. But it was a question she couldn't answer.

She was unhappy, and she thought it was my job to fix it.

As much as I struggled to please Jenny, I was having a lot more success and fun with the photography studio. One morning at 7 a.m., I was awakened by a call from my art director friend at Eison Goot. Robbin got straight to the point.

"David, how would you feel about shooting a child birth?"

I told her I wouldn't have a problem with that, and she replied "Then come on over, she's in labor!"

Turns out that arrangements had been made with a mother-to-be for photography of her delivery for use as ads for the Saint Francis Birthing Center. Hospitals were starting to promote the birth center concept over hospitalization, and this was for their first try at marketing it. The only problem was that a photographer who was a friend of the expectant mom and her family was supposed to shoot it. He'd been carrying a pager for weeks, awaiting the call that delivery was imminent. The one day he went out of town her water broke. Now they needed to go to plan B quickly. I told the AD I'd be glad to do it, but that I had another shoot at noon. By the time I got there I'd have less than three hours to shoot before leaving. I knew enough about childbirth to realize that the birth might not happen that fast. But they were stuck, and so I headed to the hospital's birthing center.

It was odd, meeting the mom in labor, her husband, her mother and her two small children as she lay in bed. She was pretty relaxed about the whole thing having been through it twice before, but the nurses did their best to protect her modesty as we all left the room whenever they checked her dilation. I was watching the clock nervously, but when they told us the baby was on the way at 11 a.m., I raced into the room with her entire family, the art director, the doctor and two nurses. Modesty was out the window as we watched the tiny head crown through the birth canal. I was doing my best to find discrete angles to shoot from, concentrating on the mom's face as the doctor reached in between her knees to pull the baby into this world. Everything went beautifully, and I even had time for shots of the mom and baby bonding and her other children meeting their new sibling before I was forced to leave for my next shoot. It was quite an experience, and the ads won me a mention in the local Addy Awards, the very first of many Addys that I received in the coming years.

If only things went that smoothly with Jenny. One evening I realized she was acting chilly towards me, and asked what was wrong.

"Oh, you KNOW. Don't tell me you don't KNOW what's wrong." I had no clue what she was referring to and told her so, but the cold shoulder continued for three days. I repeatedly asked her to tell me what I had done, but she kept repeating that I knew, and was just denying it.

When I'd finally had enough, I told her "Just tell me, I honestly have no idea what you're mad about." When she told me what the problem was I was surprised.

She said "Last week I told you I was thinking of becoming a

vegetarian, and you said forget it, because you weren't giving up meat. I was telling you I want to change my life, and you just blew me off!"

I told her I simply hadn't thought it was a serious comment. She was given to making statements about doing things that never happened, and so I replied to what I thought was an offhand remark with a similarly offhand reply. And of course, after the spat blew over, she never made any move toward becoming a vegetarian.

But that was life with Jenny.

Chapter Sixteen

Now I don't mean to make it sound like life with Jenny was always terrible. It's just that I've always been a happy go lucky guy, and it pained me that happiness just wasn't in Jenny's repertoire of emotions. I loved her and wanted her to have the same joy in life that I always felt. To her happiness came from outside, usually when she acquired something she dreamed of owning. I'd thought the spectacular new studio would keep her happy for a while, but reality never seemed to thrill her as much as dreaming of what she wanted next. When she was getting something new, she'd be happy for a little while, and then she'd feel unfulfilled again. And my job was to keep that bottomless pit of need filled.

But the next thing Jenny set her sights on turned out to be a good thing for us both.

One weekend she said "You're working too hard, you never take any time off. Let's go to the lake and look at houseboats for sale."

"Right now?" I asked.

"Yes, right now."

And so we packed up the car and drove the 40 minutes to Portman Marina on Lake Hartwell.

Jenny and I had in the past fifteen years become crazy about boats. We'd bought our first one, a 1968 Thunderbird Tri-Hull in 1983, and had spent my 30th birthday learning to ski on Lake Hartwell. One of the best vacations we'd ever had was a week spent in a tiny mobile home on the lake belonging to one of Jenny's employers, with our boat docked 50 feet from the door. We'd spent the days boating, swimming and reading, and the week had seen a substantial improvement in our normally sluggish love life. I found that nearness to the water worked wonders for her libido. But that boat was gone. I'd sold it to finance the start of our photography business in 1985, and went boatless until early in the summer of 1989. That's when Jenny dragged me to the docks at Portman Marina, insisting that I buy a boat and not work 16 hours a day until I dropped dead of a heart attack.

She'd seen an ad for a 1962 Drifter houseboat, 28 feet long with a blunt square bow and sleeping room for four people. It was just $7500., and she wanted to look at it. We drove to the marina and found the boat old, but charming, and I have to admit I liked it.

We started to walk away and I asked Jenny if she wanted to look at some more boats.

"Nope", she answered.

"Do you want to look at that one down the dock?"

"Nope."

"Do you want to think about it?"

"Nope."

"Well", I asked, "what do you want me to do, make him an offer right now!?"

"Yes." was her answer, and we became boaters again.

As we signed the papers a couple of days later, she asked me to make her a promise.

"David, I want you to promise me that you'll take some time off from work and really use this boat."

I told her I would try.

A month later she said "David, some time you have to go back to work!"

We'd gone back to boating with a vengeance, heading for the marina on Thursday and coming back to town on Tuesday. We'd spent a week on the water over the Fourth of July holiday, and hadn't spent much time at work since falling in love with the boat.

Many of the marina tenants at Portman were dock bound, rarely, if ever, taking their boats out on the 90 mile long lake. We were usually gone within 30 minutes of arriving at the dock, only returning for supplies or when it was time to head home.

We'd head down the lake to find a secluded cove, and being self employed, I could go any day of the week, when Lake Hartwell was mostly deserted. The weekends could get wild between bass fishermen and recreational boaters, but the weekdays were pretty quiet.

One summer evening we'd anchored in a quiet cove with no nearby homes, and I'd talked Jenny into trying lovemaking under the stars on the roof of the boat. We'd put beach towels over the rails to block the view in case anyone passed by, and we were both enjoying the excitement of the starry night and the freedom to be rocking on the roof of the boat as we explored each other's bodies. That came to a screeching halt as we heard a fishing boat pull up behind us, and check out the boat with their spotlight.

"Golly Vern, look at that, a houseboat out in the cove. Think it got loose and drifted here?"

His partner replied "No, I see an anchor line off the bow. Must be somebody camping out here. No lights on, maybe they're asleep."

Meanwhile, we were on the roof scrambling to keep covered by the towels that had been on the rails. We'd neglected to bring clothing to the upper deck, and the low angle of their fishing boat was the only thing keeping us from being on display. Finally they motored away, and we breathed a sigh of relief, laughing at how close we'd come to being caught in the act like teenagers.

That summer was some of the most fun boating we've ever

done, and after four months, Jenny was already wanting a bigger boat. We soon bought a 1969 vintage 52 foot SeaGoing steel hull houseboat, in need of mechanical and cosmetic work, and spent the next two years putting it in top shape. I'd always liked "boats that look like boats" not like barges or spaceships, and with its vee bottom and high pointed bow, the SeaGoing was more "boaty" than the blunt nosed Drifter. It had a kitchen with full sized refrigerator, and with a futon in the front cabin it could more comfortably sleep four adults. I became adept at the handling of the larger boat, and both of us took the US Power Squadron boating course at a local community college to learn navigation and boating skills.

The SeaGoing was a wonderful weekend boat, and we spent many a summer day cruising up and down the 90 miles of Lake Hartwell, finding quiet coves to anchor overnight. It was beautiful and quiet, and we'd only run the generator long enough to make coffee in the morning. Meals were cooked on the grill, and we swam and read novels in the sun, moving to the shady bow area when it got too hot. It was large enough for guests, and we frequently took family and other couples with us for our weekend cruises.

After a year, the 1990-91 recession had slowed our business down, and we were getting frustrated with work and the stress of dealing with clients. We gave serious thought to buying a Grand Banks trawler, which Jenny had spotted in the yachting magazines we read avidly, and moving aboard. Trawler style boats have a lot of living space, and a very classic nautical look, with teak decks and teak furnishings throughout. I dreamed we'd travel the country's waterways shooting nautical stock photography, making our living from selling it to boat magazines. We even went to Fort Lauderdale and spent a couple of days with Grand Banks dealer Hal Jones, looking at boats and falling in love with the Grand Banks style.

But my family had just moved to South Carolina, and in the end we couldn't stand the thought of being so far away. I hadn't lived in the same town with my folks for 20 years, and it had only been a year since my Mom and Dad had retired to Greenville from Chicago to be closer to us. My sister Karen and small nephew Russell had followed suit, and I was just getting used to having them close by. My brother Stephen lived in Atlanta, and it felt like the first time the whole family had been in close proximity since we'd been teenagers. Jenny & I decided to compromise, bought property 45 minutes away on Lake Hartwell, and planned to build a house with a dock there. Business picked back up, life returned to as normal as it ever got around our house, and our Grand Banks dream got put on a shelf.

Things never stayed quiet for long. We'd had the SeaGoing for a couple of years when Jenny heard that a 1969 Chris Craft houseboat was up for sale. She'd had her eye on it before we bought the SeaGoing, but the owner hadn't really wanted to sell, and wouldn't return phone calls about his "For Sale" sign. Portman Marina always seemed to have a large number of boats for sale, but many of the owners just put the signs up to see if some weekend "tire kicker" would wander by and make them an offer they couldn't refuse. The owner of the Chris Craft had let the boat deteriorate for two more years, and was finally motivated to sell it. A builder of top fuel dragsters for such names as "Big Daddy" Don Garlits, he'd kept the twin v-6 engines in good shape, but the houseboat's interior was a mess. The roof leaked, there was mildew everywhere, and the shag carpet was sodden. An unopened roll of paper towels sat on the counter, and when we picked it up it must have weighed ten pounds where moisture had soaked through it's plastic wrapping.

As we left the boat, I turned to Jenny and said "Well, I guess you're over that one, huh." Her reply surprised me.

"I want it."

"You're kidding, you see what kind of shape it's in!" I answered.

"I still want it", she insisted.

"We just spent two years fixing everything on the other boat, do you know how long this will take?!" I protested.

"I don't care, it's just the right style, and I want it."

So of course, she got it. We sold the pristine SeaGoing to a friend, moved the 34 foot Chris Craft to our slip on Dock Ten, and started ripping it apart. We hired a local boat handyman to fiberglass the roof and stop the leaking. The old Chris Crafts had thick fiberglass hulls, but the roof structure was wooden. After tearing off the vinyl on the sides he discovered rot, and we had to rip out the wall of the shower and replace a large section of the side cabin wall with new marine plywood. He started the fiberglass work while I stripped the interior to the bare walls and ceiling joists, and removed three layers of soggy carpet from the floor. I refinished the ceiling beams and put insulation and tile board between them, giving it a very nautical exposed beam look. Jenny made new curtains, and we went to the Boat US store in Atlanta, filling up two shopping carts with new radios, deck fittings, lines, fenders, galley equipment and everything else we could think of to make the boat perfect.

Five months later, it was ready to cruise. We had fun in the Chris Craft, first spending long weekends cruising from the marina, then moving it to the dock of our friend Judy. She had bought the SeaGoing houseboat from us, and the two boats shared her dock for a year while we planned our dream home on the lake, right next door to Judy's dock.

Our plans were to build a log home on the lake, and we had been surprised at what a difficult task that turned out to be. Banks consider log homes "unconventional", and I guess we should have been prepared for that. Our photography studio in Greenville was a 1929 synagogue, and getting a loan in 1988 for a young business on something that unconventional had been a struggle. Bankers generally have no imagination or vision, and the unconventional just translates into "unacceptable risk" to them. "Self employed" also translates "unemployed" to bankers who want to see a W2 form with your annual salary on it. Never mind that three of my neighbors at the lake with high dollar salaries had lost their jobs to cutbacks that summer. They had jobs, at least until they lost them!

We got increasingly frustrated at the high interest rates we were being offered, and I was feeling the pressure, mostly from self-created "deadlines" to start a project that was escalating in price.

Jenny came to my rescue this time, saying, "you know, we don't have to do this."

"Yes we do", I replied, "we've both been going crazy waiting to live on the lake property." She had an answer as usual.

"So we'll buy a boat and live on it."

"We can't do that", I said.

She came back with "Why not?"

I couldn't think of a reason, so we started looking for a boat to live on. The 34 foot Chris Craft wasn't big enough for the two of us, our four dogs and three cats, so we started looking for something economical with lots of room.

A month later, we found a 1974 Stardust cruiser that looked just right. Barge style, with a large front deck that could be used as a sun porch, the 50 foot hull needed paint, but it was a perfect liveaboard boat. It had a galley with a full size refrigerator, a head with a porcelain tub and shower, (a rarity even on large boats), and a single stateroom with two closets and a queen size bed. (Two lockers and queen sized berth, to those enamored of nautical terms). Best of all, the bunk area had been turned into a laundry, complete with washer and dryer.

The owner was a woman who lived aboard while running a boat cleaning service on Lake Lanier near Atlanta. She'd retired from a career roaming the world as a crew person on large yachts, but didn't want to be too far away from boats. Holiday Marina on Lanier was a perfect place for her, with a large number of boats with bright work in constant need of varnish. One of her clients was the owner of a classic Chris Craft commuter that had once belonged to Humphrey Bogart, and it had about an acre of varnished wood. She puttered around the marina in her Boston Whaler with cleaning and varnishing supplies, taking care of her steady clients. Now she'd bought a larger boat to live on, and the older Stardust was for sale.

We bought it, and arranged for a tractor trailer to haul it the 100 miles from Lanier to Lake Hartwell. A week later I had my first experience as it's captain when I took it from the
docks to the launch ramp, and drove it up onto the flatbed cradle.

I'd assumed the delivery driver would put it on the truck, but he said "It's your boat, you drive it on there."

He and I spent four hours removing the flying bridge atop the boat so that it would clear the interstate bridges, and we followed along behind the truck as our boat made it's way North towards it's new home.

After getting it back in the waters of Lake Hartwell, reassembled, cleaned and painted, we moved aboard with our four dogs and three cats for what we planned as a one year break from land. That first year, I didn't care if the house ever got built.

Living on the water was wonderful, watching the Blue Herons fish on the beach while drinking my morning coffee, walking outside for a swim before making the 45 minute commute to work, listening to the splash of the beaver at night. Of course there were drawbacks, too. Carrying groceries down the 95 steps on the steep hill, and carrying garbage 95 steps back up. Freezing in the winter, despite adding storm windows, four electric heaters and an electric blanket. Under the blanket at night was the only time that winter we were truly warm.

Then there were the "Bass assholes". That's what we called the rude fisherman who haunted our cove, along with the rest of the lake. They'd cast their lures at the boat, hitting the steel hull and making it clang, then deny it when confronted. One morning I was sitting in the booth in the boat's kitchen, when two fishermen pulled up next to the window and started staring in.

"Golly Vern, will you look at that, they've got a full-sized refrigerator in that boat!"

It was like I wasn't even there.

I went outside and asked them, "How would you like it if I pulled to the end of your driveway, parked there, stared into your windows and commented on your furniture?"

"Huh?' was their reply.

When I told them we'd appreciate a little privacy, I got the usual "We've got just as much right as you do to be here." A little courtesy would have been nice though.

Also, difficult was the lack of "our stuff". Most of our

possessions were in storage, and we made weekly trips to the storage building to try and find things we needed or to get rid of things we didn't have room for on the boat. We were working, not cruising, so we still needed a work wardrobe, and not much would fit on the boat. I built a walk-in closet at the studio, and would frequently have to change into something more appropriate than shorts and tee shirt after getting to work.

After the first year on the boat, we were getting tired of being cramped and of having seven animals underfoot, so we finally started our log home. The builder had estimated a four to six months construction schedule, but he hadn't taken into account the rainy winter or the massive foundation required by the steep hill. Eleven months and a lot of gray hair later, we finally moved into our new home. The day after, they broke ground for our carport! After one full year of construction, the workers left and we settled into life on land. We'd lived for two full years on the boat, and while I was ready for that period to end, I hoped someday we'd live aboard again, this time without the constraints of a landlocked lake and a daily work schedule.

Living on the boat during the construction of the log home was an adventure all it's own. If there's one thing a contractor hates, it's having the owner live at the construction site. I had warned Gary, the builder, that this was my dream home, it had been in the planning stages for years, and that I was "Very picky." He assured me that as a builder of log homes, he was used to picky owners, and that it was not a problem for him. I'd gotten the idea for a log home years earlier, and had seen the Southland Log Homes model beside I-26 in Columbia, SC on my travels. I stopped in for a brochure, and decided it was the home for me. It seemed like the ultimate tree house to a grownup kid, and I'd spent more than a few years living out my childhood dreams of boats, romance, fun cars and unique homes. My residences had included a barrel shaped duplex with a spiral staircase, a 150 year old plantation house surrounded with magnolias, a contemporary home with high peaked roof and an outdoor shower that had been my first studio, the synagogue and later the houseboat. Now I was ready for my next adventure, and I envisioned living in it until retirement.

    I met with the owner of Southland Log Homes, and pitched an idea to him. I'd photograph log homes for his advertising and marketing, and trade for the cost of the log home package, about $30,000. worth of materials. He wasn't willing to be out of pocket on the materials, and we compromised, starting with a $5,000. credit for the first batch of home photos. Log homes are extremely difficult to photograph, located often in heavily wooded locations and with their dark tones, wide shadowing porches and difficult angles. Southland was impressed with the architectural photography I'd done, and was willing to give me a try. After six months of scattered shooting, we'd used up the first allotment and extended the trade two more times. I kept shooting log homes for the next year, using the experience of seeing many completed homes to learn more and more about what worked and what didn't.

Jenny and I picked out a stock floor plan, and made numerous changes to it with the Southland experts turning them into blueprints. Our suggestions went over so well that Southland later made our changes into a stock plan.

When the day came in the fall to deliver the log package, we were really excited. The logs would be stored under tarps on the building site, like parts of a giant jigsaw puzzle. All of the doors, flooring, windows and interior finish wood was stored in a nearby rental storage facility. I had envisioned the construction being at a stage where the logs immediately started going up, but the foundation work had been slowed by an unplanned change. Seems the builder had made his budget with only a cursory look at the site, and by the time the measurements and plans were drawn, the 8 foot high basement became twelve feet of solid concrete, filled with rebar, sending the budget soaring. It had also taken much longer than anticipated, and we were now into the winter rainy season. It was painful for me, watching my piles of very expensive logs sitting under tarps in the rain and wind, constantly checking them for water damage. Things dragged through the winter, with me becoming more and more impatient, until they finally started assembling the logs in the spring. The builder felt things were progressing quickly at that point, but I told him the problem was that the months long delays had "used up all of my patience." I watched every day before going to the studio as the logs were lifted into place, and the walls started to rise.

When work started on the second level, the flooring being

put into place was two inch thick pine boards which also formed the ceiling of the lower level. I cautioned the carpenters to not use any bad boards, as I didn't want knotholes or warps or splits in either my floor or ceiling. A few hours later, I got a call from the builder, Gary.

"David, I just spoke with the carpenters, and only about 20 percent of the wood for the floors are up to your specs." I didn't see how that was possible, and jumped in my van for the long ride to the lake. As the carpenters showed me the collection of what I saw as flawed boards, I had to agree, they would not do.

I called Southland, and was told "Those are #2 grade pine boards, not #1. They are allowed a certain number of knotholes and imperfections. It's what's in your contract."

I protested that it was unsuitable for flooring, and was told most people who installed it in the upper floors put carpet over it.

That seemed like a waste of lumber to me, but I was told, "Hey, that's what #2 lumber looks like. If you want to come here and take a look and see if you can find some betters boards, you're welcome to try."

They obviously didn't know my personality.

The next day I rented a U-Haul trailer, loaded up the 80% of the boards I found flaws in, and drove the 100 miles to Columbia. I had measured the longest board to be sure it would fit in the trailer, but found that when the door was closed, it was an inch too short. I had to put the stacks in diagonally to make them fit so that I could close the door, and they were stacked to the top of the trailer. Shortly before reaching Columbia, I bounced over a railroad crossing, and heard a large bang from the trailer. I pulled over to the side and checked the trailer, and the boards had fallen off their pile, creating a bulge in the roll up door. I tried to open it to check the load, but the door was stuck fast. On arrival at Southland I was directed to a storage shed stacked with bundles of flooring boards. The workers tried to help me open the door of the trailer, but it took 30 minutes of pounding with a sledgehammer before we managed to get it open. Then I spent four hours sorting through bundles of lumber until I had swapped all of my boards for pristine pine. It was backbreaking labor, but I ended up with a beautiful floor and ceiling.

As the shell of the house was finished, the interior work got underway. When the framing of the stairwell started, I walked in and immediately saw that the landing was too tall. And, they were power nailing the boards into place on my beautiful log walls. I pointed out the error to the carpenter, who got very testy with me.

"I know what I'm doing, this is the right spot", he said. I insisted he measure again. The landing was about a foot too tall, and would have put the stairs ending an inch or two from the front door. I'd saved him a lot of work, and the builder money, as they hadn't even cut the risers yet. But they didn't see it that way. Soon I got a phone call from the builder.

"David, you've got to leave them alone and let them do their job!"

I protested that I saved time, materials and damage to the log walls by catching the mistake early, but he was unconvinced.

"You need to let us catch our own mistakes", he insisted.

The mistakes continued, and when it involved damage to my logs, I intervened as soon as I spotted the problems. One wall was being framed into the wrong spot by over a foot on the hall bath. The room would have been too narrow to even put a toilet in. In the hallway upstairs, they were putting the door frames in the wrong spot, and I stopped that. In one upstairs room, the ceiling was supposed to be exposed beams, and I came home to find a lower ceiling framed in. It was all ripped out the next day. At least the builder was fixing the problems, but it had become a frustrating experience for me.

One of the biggest issues had been my desire to protect as many trees as possible. The home was being built on a heavily wooded lot, and I was not willing to lose the giant hardwoods. Most builders prefer to scalp a large clearing for the construction, putting small trees and bushes back when they are finished, but I convinced Gary that saving my big trees was important. We put marking tape on all of the trees to be saved, including the towering oak that came through the porch and roofline next to the dining room.

Gary questioned me, saying "What will you do if that tree dies after you've built everything around it?"

I told him I'd "Cut it off above the roof line, and it will look from the house like it's still there."

And that is actually what happened. Three years after moving in, the tree was struck by lightning, peeling a strip of bark four inches wide and twenty-five feet long from the tree, ending at the roofline. From there the lightning headed indoors, taking out the phones, TV and hot water heater. The bolt killed the tree, and I had it cut off just above the porch roof. The loggers took the main body of the tree down in one cut, shaking the neighborhood and putting cracks in my basement floor.

As my dream log home finally approached completion, the site foreman, who openly disliked me for my perceived interference with his crew, came to me with a request. He was ready to backfill around the foundation, and wanted to cut down all of the trees around it to get in a backhoe for the work. I was appalled at this suggestion, and reminded him that the builder, his boss, had agreed to preserve the trees. Now as the house neared completion, he wanted me to allow him to cut them down after nearly a year of working around them. I refused, and told him there was no way he was cutting those trees.

"Then how do you expect me to backfill this 12 foot high foundation?" he shouted at me.

"I don't care if you have to use shovels, you're not cutting down my trees!" I shouted back at him.

The supervisor called his boss in a rage, and when the builder backed me up on not cutting the trees, he quit and walked off the job.

They filled in the foundation with shovels.

Chapter Seventeen

Sunday, November 21st

We awoke to fog, and had to wait a few minutes as it cleared, but we were still away from the dock by 6:30 a.m. We had talked the previous night with the owner of Ahrtyme, a 42' Marine Trader out of Winter Park, Florida, and he had briefly tried running outside in the Atlantic last night at 11 p.m. The forecast of three foot seas turned out to be four to five foot seas, and just past the jetties a big wave tore a chunk out of his stern rail. He decided that was way too rough, and turned around and ran the boat back inside to the sheltered waters. Most everyone we've talked to on the trip that has run on the outside has decided it wasn't worth the beating they were taking and headed back to the ICW. As we headed South, Cap ragged me all morning on my "descriptive" navigating, as he read the charts while I steered.

He told me to " Meander left, but not too far, and then a

gentle sweeping turn to the right, not too close to the red marker, but then not too far either."

He likes to pick on me, but when I tell him "Head for the red" Rick then wants more detail! Hard to find that happy medium, and at night I err on the side of TMI. We've run aground several times from not having enough info. While I was below making us tea Cap pounded on the roof, and when I came up to the bridge he pointed out seven endangered White Pelicans on a sand bar next to us. We crossed the shipping channel in the Saint John's River at 8:50, where I shot a weird looking barge with three fins. My Dad had lived in Jacksonville growing up and spent a lot of his childhood playing on the St. Johns, steering a tiny sailboat in and out of the giant cargo ships making their way downriver. It was nice passing through a piece of family history.

At 9:05 it was looking like rain, but we were hoping it would hold off, as driving the boat on the flybridge in the rain is a miserable experience. When we'd started this cruise in Maryland it had been bitterly cold, but we were pretty comfortable in the balmier Florida weather as long as it stayed dry. At 12:30 we entered Saint Augustine harbor, past Castillo San Marcos, a Spanish fort built in 1672. It's the oldest masonry fort in the US, a reminder of how dangerous Florida had been for the earliest settlers. We cruised under the famous "Bridge of Lions" with its huge feline statues at 12:45. I took a few shots of 'Anastasia', a paddle wheeler sitting by the riverbank, looking like it belonged in another era.

At 2 p.m. we went under the Crescent City Bridge, and by 5 were passing Ormond by the Sea. That was a place Jenny and I had spent a fun weekend, staying in a seedy motel that reminded me of Florida in the late 50's, and finding a huge bronze porthole in a junk shop that I later installed in the front of my log home on the lake. The day's run had been pleasant, with good depth along straight scenic channels as we passed through Cabbage Swamp. The only hitch besides the clouds and the constant threat of rain was the fact that almost no one obeys the No Wake zones. I saw skiers in NW zones, and most boats just blasted past us with a casual wave, rocking us all afternoon.

By late afternoon it had started sprinkling, and as it got dark the rain and wind picked up. By 6:30 it was pretty rough, and we were struggling to keep the charts dry and pick up the marks in the rain. We'd planned on running until at least 9 p.m., but by 7 p.m. we were ready to head for shelter. The first marina we pulled up to had such shallow depth that the falling tide would have left us sitting in the mud. I went below to try and identify our location and find the nearest docking, which turned out to be Halifax Marina. It's very large, but when we called on the radio they said they were completely full. They sent us to Daytona Marina, and we called and were told they had room. After running aground a couple of times in the wind and the dark, we found the narrow entrance channel and Cap fought the wind and tide to make the turn into our berth.

We dried off and went to the Chart House restaurant

overlooking the dock, where we had a good but overpriced meal, sitting next to some really loud and obnoxious millionaires talking about blowing $1,800. on dinner for four, people who leave $25,000. tips and the various clinics they'd been in and out of to get sober. One talked of stupid things like buying a boat when he was too drunk to remember it, running it on a bank and leaving it there, only later finding out he owned it! Money sure can't buy happiness or good taste. I was relieved when they left. After dinner I took my first shower since our stop in Charleston last Thursday, and it felt great. Cap and I took turns doing laundry at the dockside laundromat, our first chance to catch up on it since Bellhaven the previous Monday. I was asleep by 12:30 that night, tired but clean. We'd traveled 113 miles today, 872 for the trip. I was starting to believe I'd be home for Thanksgiving.

Rick had been intrigued when I'd told him about the bronze porthole I'd put in my new home, and I couldn't resist telling him about my plans for the entrance. The porthole, with its inch thick glass, was to the left of the front door, and two bronze caged lights from a Japanese freighter flanked the door. I'd always hated bland doors, feeling that when you knock on the front door, that's the first impression of the home's construction. But I went a little overboard, and ordered a custom mahogany slab with a circular motif on it to match the feel of the porthole. The builder had been terrified of working on the $2,000. piece of wood, and made me watch as he chiseled spots for the heavy hinges and drilled out a spot for the latch and lock. Inside, I had made a trade with a client who I had photographed custom staircases for. I'd traveled the Southeast shooting his curving freestanding stairs in mansions for marketing use, and I traded more photos to have him build me a mahogany newel post with the same design as the front door. I planned on living in this house a long time, and I had obsessed over every detail.

During the previous year, I'd had the good fortune to shoot a project that had inspired the circular motif of the door. I was contacted by an interior designer who was handling the decor of the new Greer Commission of Public Works headquarters in suburban Greenville, and she was looking to commission art to hang on the walls. I was excited as we talked, and her initial suggestion was photos of their facilities. I quickly agreed, and after working out budgets, began a tour of their facilities around the county. I envisioned heroic images of giant public works projects, much like Margaret Bourke White's iconic image of the Fort Peck Dam on the cover of the first issue of Life Magazine back in 1936, but the reality turned out to be somewhat different.

Unfortunately their facilities were small, and didn't lend themselves to the kind of images I imagined. I went back to the drawing board, and came up with the idea of shooting abstract images that would suggest the facilities rather than show the buildings. I shot tight angles of electric meters stacked together, very close up images of conduit being installed in a water plant, macro geometrical patterns of dried sludge in a sewage yard and my favorite, a large round metal fitting for a sewer plant under construction. I'd been walking towards another spot in the site with my 4x5 view camera on a tripod when my assistant Carla pointed out the pipe behind me. I loved the dramatic view of the pipe, with the rest of the construction receding out behind it like the view through a lens, and it was the best piece of the display. I always gave Carla credit for spotting it.

When I met with the Greer Board of Commissioners to present the work before the large prints were made and framed, I was a little nervous about how they would react. This was a group of public servants, not art lovers, and I worried that the abstract images might not be what they were expecting. They sure surprised me. I was showing black and white 8x10's to represent the large 30x40 prints that would be hung, and color slides of the other dozen 16x20 images to be hung between them.

When an image shot with a wide angle of a vivid yellow gas meter against a deep blue sky from ground level came up on the screen, I noticed there was a fly on the meter. Projected on the boardroom wall that fly was a couple of inches in size, and I was embarrassed not to have noticed it in my editing. I told the board "Don't worry about the fly on the meter, I have other frames without it."

"Leave the fly, we love it!" was their response. They loved everything, and at the building's grand opening a couple of months later, they held an unveiling of the exhibit on the 80 foot long curved wall of the lobby. Employees stood around trying to guess which of the images were from which facility, and the reception was a hit. The first thing you see walking in their building is the gas meter shot by the front door, the fly proudly atop his perch. Twenty years later, the display still hangs there.

Back at the lake, the home of my dreams was finally nearing completion. We were still living on the houseboat as construction wound down, and we would pay one more price for that adventure.

Jenny had been a collector of pets, and we were living on the 400 square foot boat with Molly the Rottweiler, McGee the elderly Corgi, Heather, another Corgi and Mouse, an adorably tiny miniature Pinscher, along with three cats, named Ansel Adams, Annie Leibovitz and Munchie. The dogs hopped on and off the boat to the dock constantly, and I'd warned Jenny numerous times to block them in the boat when she wasn't there. Every wake that went by rocked the boat and the dock, and though the gap was just a few inches, it could pull away as the dock lines strained against the moorings with the passing waves. Her response to my warnings was always the same. "Don't be ridiculous, dogs are born great swimmers, even if they fall in, they'll just swim to shore! You are such a worrier." I knew how hard it would be on her if we lost one of them to an accident, but she wouldn't listen. The call came from a neighbor one day while I was at the studio. "David, you have to come home right now, McGee fell in the water, and he's not breathing! Jenny is hysterical." I left right away, but by the time I'd made the 40 minute drive to the lake, McGee had been buried by a neighbor in the front yard of our unfinished home. My wife was inconsolable in her loss, but we never talked about how he died. I never said "I told you so", and she never took responsibility for leaving him alone on the dock after all my warnings not to.

Now it was fall in South Carolina, and the log home on the lake was finally ready to move in. We'd hoped to celebrate our 20th anniversary in 1994 in our new home in early October, but the builder missed that deadline by a couple of weeks. The joy of anniversaries seemed to matter more to me than to Jenny, and this one was no exception. I always felt it was a celebration of our time together, building a life and surviving the trials and tribulations, but my romantic ideas didn't always appeal to Jenny.

When we'd celebrated our first anniversary together in 1975 as I toiled driving the bread truck, I'd wanted a special way to mark the occasion. A card just didn't seem like enough. Walking around the old campus at the University of Georgia I'd spotted a wooden bench with a brass plaque on the back. Looking closer, I read "On this bench, I asked Suzie to marry me. And she said yes," along with the date of their marriage. I thought that was terrifically romantic, but since I'd asked Jenny to marry me in a spur of the moment proposal as we sat on the curb of my old elementary school, I didn't have a great place to put a plaque. Instead, I had one engraved with the date of our first anniversary, and the words "You put the meaning into my life", and mounted it on a walnut backing. When I'd first given it to her all those years ago, she'd been moved to tears. Now, after getting a new plaque annually for the past 20 years, she was bored with them.

We'd moved around so much in the last few years that they hadn't all been hung on the wall in a long time, and when I announced my intention to put all 20 of them on our new bedroom wall, she objected. "It will take up so much room." she complained. Not exactly the response I'd hoped for. I insisted on hanging them, and every woman who visited our house in the next few years and saw the display declared it "The most romantic thing I've ever seen." Some of the engravings were poems, some lyrics from songs, but one of my favorites was from our third anniversary, when we were struggling to work out our differences and stay married. I'd written "Though the waters may at times get rough, still we sail on, together." The running joke prior to our 20th anniversary had been that the year's plaque should be "Although the water may at times get rough, at least we bought a bigger boat!"

And so things rocked along, with me working harder and harder to support the lake house and Jenny's desired life style, and with her seldom showing up at work. She always seemed to have an excuse for not coming in to the studio, from headaches to chores, organizing the house to grocery shopping, and she was less and less involved in the photography business. I wasn't complaining too much about her not working, as things were going great in my photography studio. I was traveling the country, shooting work for hospitals and colleges in New York and the

Northeast, as far West as California, and even a couple of shoots in Canada.

I discovered light painting, using a Xenon powered fiber optic light through a flexible hose to create other worldly effects on film before the days of Photoshop, and used it on many high profile and lucrative projects. The first big light painting project was a corporate brochure for Mount Vernon Mills. My friend Kimberley had created a stunning design for the piece describing the workings of making fabrics for the Greenville based company, and she wanted me to do the photography. The many large images of textile equipment were indicated in the layout with large X's, and it was my privilege to make them come to life in vibrant colors. We traveled throughout South Carolina and to Georgia, Alabama and Texas to find the right machinery to photograph at Mount Vernon's many textile mills, spending as much as 15 hours on a single image. With light painting the photographs were created on a 4x5 View camera in near darkness, so we were building blackout tents the size of 18 wheelers in the plants to work inside. It was an exhausting three weeks of traveling and shooting, but I've always considered it some of my finest work.

In 1996 I was feeling that the Crosby Images name was a little dated. The years of shooting with film crews who always called me "The stills guy" as in "We're ready for stills." made me think of becoming Crosby Stills, and Jenny had been pushing for it. My resistance was that I thought people might consider it some fan tribute to Crosby, Stills and Nash. They're still one of my favorite bands, but not a reason to change business names. It was the early days of the world wide web, and when I found that www.crosbystills.com was available I was finally convinced. I'd discovered that every time we changed web hosts we ended up with new e-mail addresses, making us harder to find. My new e-mail of david@crosbystills.com has now been a constant for almost two decades.

My staff had a lot of fun with the name change announcement for the studio. We wanted to do something fun, and George and Vanessa came up with the idea of illustrating how we were "changing images", as Crosby Images became Crosby Stills. I'm known for my laid back, soft spoken persona, so they went shopping for a black leather vest, leather biker gloves, and a leather and silver studded dog collar to dress me in. The pose was in black and white, me with a clenched fist, a mean glare and a Crosby Stills logo tattoo Photoshopped on my bicep. It was all we could do to get through the shoot for the laughter, and it was a hit with the clients. They loved the name as much as the announcement.

Vanessa was my third long time assistant, something I'd been known for in Greenville. Virtually all of the other area photographers had male assistants, but I'd always been comfortable working with women, starting with Marilyn, my first part-time assistant. When she left I'd hired Carla to work full-time, and three years later when Carla departed I hired Vanessa.

Vanessa had traveled with me more than the others, as she was my assistant when Jenny began to pull back from work all together.

The jobs that year included photographing sports cars for BMW, a motorhome on a cliff in Utah for Michelin, and the US Olympic Kayak Team on a river in Colorado for Perception Kayaks. Life was fun, and I was trying to keep Jenny happy, so if she didn't want to come to work, it wasn't worth fighting about. Of course, even that could get complicated. I was having to stay late at work doing the office work when Jenny didn't show up, and when I told my assistant Vanessa that I was thinking of hiring a bookkeeper, she asked me if she could take on the job. Vanessa was tired of assisting, and proposed that she start shooting her own projects while taking over the bookkeeping duties. That way I could use the savings to hire another assistant. I thought it sounded great, and assumed Jenny would be thrilled. Boy was I wrong.

When I came home that evening, she was on the porch smoking. She walked out to the driveway, and I couldn't wait to tell her about the new plan. It meant no more pressure to come to work for her, giving her the free time she claimed to need. Her response was immediate.

"You've fired me. You and Vanessa have gotten together and fired me!"

I told her, no, I was just trying to free her from an obligation she seemed to dislike, but there was no calming her down.

The more I assured her no one was firing her, the more agitated she became.

Near the end of the confrontation, she shrieked at me at the top of her lungs "You F**king FIRED me!"

I was worried the neighbors would call the police at that point, and walked inside the house to escape. The ironic thing was that in spite of her loud protest, she seldom came to the office after that, and Vanessa started doing the bookkeeping. In typical Jenny fashion, she wanted the title, but not the work that went with it.

Things calmed down, and life got back to as normal as it ever was. Then Jenny surprised me with an uncharacteristically generous impulse. I'd been driving Chevy vans for years, using them to haul the ever growing collection of gear that I used on location shoots. With the advent of light painting, I was hauling a dozen large cases, and was struggling to pack it all into the van. We worked off of rolling carts, but the loading and unloading process was tedious and slow, and I started shopping for a work truck for the studio. I found an Isuzu NPR truck for sale that looked perfect. It had a 14 foot cargo box behind the tilting cab and a rollup door, and I had a 1,000 pound lift gate added as part of the purchase. I had giant sized Crosby Stills logos installed on the sides, paneled and decorated the inside of the cargo box, even refinishing the hardwood flooring, and built a corner closet that could double as a model's dressing room and a film loading room. After purchasing a larger rolling cart and building a box on it with compartments for the lighting gear, we had the ultimate in mobile grip trucks. And there was one more benefit. I didn't need to drive a van anymore.

My love of sports cars had started as a child when my Dad would stop by Baker Motors in Atlanta after church on Sunday where we would look at sports cars. They sold everything from MG's to Lamborghinis, and I grew up with a passion for sporty foreign cars. In my senior year of high school I had traded in my VW bus for a beautiful little Austin Healy Sprite, my first convertible. Since then my cars had included a Mazda RX7 and a Porsche 924, but the car of my dreams had always been a Porsche 911, and I decided to find a used one in my budget.

Jenny surprised me by being all for it, even telling me that "You deserve it."

And so my search started, looking at every used 911 anywhere near Greenville, SC. Then I widened the search to Columbia, and then Charlotte, NC, and even to Atlanta, all with no luck. The only 911's close to my $20,000. budget were junky or needed work. One was even rusted out. Now in the 1990's, $20,000 was a lot of money for a used car, but apparently still not enough for a used Porsche 911 in decent shape. Discouraged after nearly a month of searching, and getting tired of commuting 35 miles daily to the lake house in the huge truck, I was frustrated and running out of options. On the way home from dinner one night during one of Jenny's rare trips to Greenville, we passed the Jaguar dealer, who had a shiny black BMW Z3 on his lot.

Jenny said "How about that car?"

I answered that "I probably can't afford it anyway", but we pulled in to look at it.

The dealer said he was about to close, but let me sit in it for a minute, encouraging me to come back the next day. It was beautiful. Only two years old with 27,000 miles on it, it reminded me of an MGB from my youth but with more creature comforts added. They were asking $24,000., but as we drove away that night, I told Jenny that if they would come down to $22,000. I'd buy it. I took my assistant and friend George with me the next day, because he's a tough negotiator and knew I was in love with the car. He got me the price I wanted, including a new set of tires, and the next day I picked it up. I drove back to my synagogue studio with the top down, and my employees stood on the front steps cheering as I drove up. Over the next seven years I put 100,000 miles on what my staff called "the Batmobile" and had a blast with it. And I got over wanting a 911. Encouraging me to buy the Z3 was one of the nicest things Jenny ever did for me.

And life was good again for a while.

Chapter Eighteen

Monday, November 22nd

Up at 5:30 a.m. again, I felt a little rough. Five hours sleep just wasn't quite enough. We left the Daytona Marina dock at 6:30, and Captain Rick had me back the boat from the dock by some very close yachts, turn around a corner past a 65 foot Hatteras and then swing it out into the marina entrance channel in the dark. A little nerve wracking. The sun rose to a pretty sky just after the rain, but it was still cloudy with more rain threatening. We hoped it would hold off, so that we could make good time today. The plan was to pick Rick's wife up in Stuart before lunchtime the next day. We passed Pelican rookeries covered with hundreds of birds, a large Man o war, and we saw the New Smyrna lighthouse in the distance. A large Sea Ray cabin cruiser with a young lady with a big smile that Cap remembered from our brief stop at Golden Isles Marina passed us at 8:30.

Then look out! "Good Time Charlie" is on his way. Put up the breakables and secure the boat for a tidal wave. We heard him asking the dockmaster at Halifax for assistance getting away from the dock, and sure enough, over the vhf we hear the call and the dockmasters comment.

"Do you know where the No Wake zone is? Well you're in it!" Good Time Charlie must be getting close. He passed us at 9:30, waving happily as we bounced through his wake. The sailboat in front of us was not so lucky, getting bounced so badly they lost control and were sideways in the channel, mast bobbing like a cork.

They called "Good Time jerk!" over the radio as he faded into the distance, oblivious to the damage he causes.

When they came alongside us, Captain Rick told them they'd probably find things below they hadn't seen in years. They were surprised to hear that this was our fourth encounter with Charlie, as he ran fast but stopped much earlier than we did, passing us again the following day.

We passed through the long chain of islets in Mosquito Lagoon, where I wondered at the big building in the distance. Turned out to be the Vehicle Assembly Building and Shuttle Hangers at Cape Canaveral, and we could see the shuttle being fueled on the launch pad as we drew closer.

I asked if you could hear it take off from this distance, and Capt. Rick laughed, saying "It makes such a roar it shakes the ground and you have to cover your ears."

We passed under the NASA Causeway Bridge, and at the end of the Lagoon, we turned into the Haulover, a short canal connecting us to the Indian River. I'd seen photos of tugs dragging used Shuttle boosters through the canal back to the Kennedy Space Center for refurbishment. We had our first bottlenose dolphin playing in the wake of the Gibbous, turning first to bathe one side in the wake and then the other, his own personal dolphin Jacuzzi! At 11 a.m. we passed an enormous dredging barge, with dredge pipes connected together front and rear to two tugs. It was so long, we weren't sure how it could make the narrow twists and turns of the channel. The rest of the day was uneventful, filled with the sights of waterfront homes and slow moving sailboats, punctuated by the occasional speeding powerboat throwing their wakes over us all. We spent the night at a small marina in Vero Beach, tired from the hours of waves and wakes. We'd made 123 miles for the day, which wasn't bad with all of the bridge openings we'd waited on. Our total mileage for the trip was 995, with a little more than 300 miles still to go.

Over dinner aboard, Captain Rick asked about my previous traveling and was surprised when I told him of Jenny's phobias about travel. At the time we moved into the lake house, Jenny had given up doing any assisting on local shoots, but had still been willing to do some of the regional out of town trips. We were friends with a client and her boyfriend in Augusta, and they liked for me to bring Jenny along on hospital shoots in their area so that we could all socialize after work.

David Crosby

Kay-Lynn was a director, and we'd worked together on a number of TV commercials, including a large project to shoot a beautiful commercial in some 150 foot sand dunes at Silver Lake, Michigan. After three days hiking the dunes together and watching her direct the Panavision film, we were all fast friends. Kay-Lynn had announced that after the editing was done, the four of us would travel to St. Barts in the French West Indies, and rent a villa for a week. Jenny was resistant, as her travel phobia combined with her fear of flying in small planes made this a trip she could not get excited about, but Kay-Lynn persisted. I did a lot of research on the kind of plane, and the one in the brochures was a 20 passenger Otter STOL (short takeoff and landing). It sounded safe and not too scary for her, and Jenny reluctantly agreed to go.

She'd been paranoid about small planes ever since I'd taken her on a flight to Athens, Georgia, for a Bulldogs football game. I was shooting the game for a newspaper, and she wanted to visit friends from my college days while I worked. The paper had always chartered a sleek twin engine plane, and when I arrived at the airport and discovered the tiny and elderly Piper they had booked for me, it was too late for her to back out. The game ran long, traffic backed up at the small Athens Airport, and we flew back to Columbus, Georgia, in the dark, soon running into a violent thunderstorm. Jenny sat in the back seat biting her nails nervously, and when the pilot started banging at a stuck gauge on the dash, fiddling with wires underneath it and finally staring out the window at the wing, I was nervous and she was in tears.

We landed without a problem, but she declared on the spot she'd never go on a small plane again. Now she had been talked into it.

The trip to St. Barts started with a commercial jet flight to San Juan, Puerto Rico, where we met Kay-Lynn and Dave. We went to the charter gate, and began looking for the 20 passenger Otter. Surprise, we were booked on a six passenger plane! Jenny protested, but she was stuck at this point, and not a happy camper as the pilot helped her climb onto the wing to get aboard. The three hour flight was pretty and uneventful, passing over chains of islands as we made our way to our destination. As we neared St. Barts, we could see the pretty harbor of Gustavia with yachts at anchor, hotels and villas rising up the sides of the volcanic mountains. But we didn't see an airstrip.

We started heading for a high mountain with a narrow ridge road winding atop it, coming closer, closer, until we were just a few feet off the ground. When the plane suddenly dove off the cliff behind the ridge and plunged straight down all four of us screamed, certain a crash was imminent. The pilot then pulled the nose up near the ground before gliding to a smooth landing. The pilot had neglected to tell us that the airport at St. Barts is built into the cliff, with the runway backing up to it and ending in the bay on the other side. You can't approach from the bayside, because overshooting the runway would mean crashing into the mountain. The planes takeoff towards the bay, but the only way to land is to come as close to the ridge as possible and dive off it before landing. Turns out it's so entertaining to watch that the locals spend their afternoons at the airport watching the landings and the rattled passengers arriving. A common problem is that the cloth topped jeeps which are the only cars on the island frequently have airplane landing gears punch through their tops as they meet on the ridge.

St. Barts was amazing, and our villa on the mountainside overlooked a beautiful bay on the back side of the island, away from the small town on the front side. We had our own pool, and hiked to the beach on the cliff side to lay on the sand and swim. One day the four of us chartered a catamaran from a French couple, who took us to nearby Goat Island to swim and explore. They anchored the big cat out in the cove, and we all jumped into the water to swim to the deserted rock covered island and it's population of appropriately enough, goats. As soon as we jumped in, Jenny shouted that she'd lost her contact lens. It was a permanent style lens, and she was lost without it. Amazingly, Kay-Lynn poked her hand out of the water with the lens atop her fingertip, and shouted "I've got it!" The two of them swam back to the boat, and Dave and I announced that we'd swim on in to the island. We swam and swam, and suddenly realized we were still a long way from shore. When we looked back, we were a long way from the boat too. Dave's a pretty weak swimmer, and while I do ok, I'm no lifesaver. I was afraid if Dave got into trouble he could drag us both under. I told him, "Stay calm, let's take our time and we'll be fine."

We got to shore without incident, where we were fascinated

with the rounded gray rocks speckled with white that covered the shore, so of course we picked up many of the prettiest small ones, putting them in our pockets. Kay-Lynn had joined us by this time, although Jenny stayed on the boat, still dealing with her contact lens. When we started back to the boat, Dave and I quickly realized pockets full of rocks was a VERY bad idea, and emptied them back in to the sea. But there was one five pound rock the shape and size of an ostrich egg that I just couldn't part with. I kept it in my left hand as I swam, stroking the water with my right, and was of course making slow progress. My two friends got farther and farther ahead of me as they approached the boat, and Jenny could see I was struggling.

She was worried I would go under, and as I finally neared the boarding ladder, she leaned out and shouted "Give me your hand!"

I reached up and answered breathlessly "Take the rock."

When she saw the huge rock in my hand she yelled "Are you nuts?!"

It was a comical moment, but I hadn't wanted to part with my souvenir, and was glad I'd made it to the boat. The rock still sits on my desk, a reminder of a wonderful week in St. Barts, French West Indies.

The trip was great, but Jenny was more convinced than ever that travel was not for her. After moving into the log home, she'd announced that her assisting days were over. From now on, I could take someone else, she wasn't going. Travel had always been iffy with Jenny. Our first trip to New York had been so much fun but ended with an argument over a wrong turn, and she had gone with me to the annual Photo Expo in Manhattan only once more. The first two years we'd stayed at the funky and artsy Chelsea Hotel, famous for being where Sid Vicious killed his girlfriend Nancy, and it currently was the home of numerous arts luminaries. But it was rough around the edges, and I told Jenny that for the next year, we'd move uptown. I booked a room in a swank Park Avenue hotel, and we made our plans. The very day of departure, Jenny dropped a bomb.

"I'm just not ready. You go, and I'll meet you there tomorrow."

I was very unhappy, but she wouldn't listen, and assured me she'd arrive tomorrow. For the next three days, the phone call was the same.

"I'm just not ready, maybe tomorrow."

Until the last day, when she finally acknowledged that she wasn't coming at all. A lot of money wasted on that Park Avenue hotel room.

The trip was a big success for me in spite of Jenny's absence, and with an added bonus. One of the seminar speakers was musician Graham Nash, himself an accomplished photographer and owner of Nash Images, a company that was instrumental in developing digital printing technology. As a fan of Crosby, Stills, Nash and sometimes Young, I've seen the band in concert a few times, and frequently got kidded about having the same name as band leader David Crosby. I got the chance to chat with Graham about the approaching digital revolution after his presentation, and it led to a funny exchange.

After talking a few minutes he leaned in and said "I'm sorry, I didn't catch your name."

I said "It's David Crosby."

He looked annoyed, said "Yeah right." and resumed his chatting about digital technology.

I pointed to my seminar name badge and said "No, that's really my name."

He laughed and said "That's too funny! I'll have to tell Croz next time I see him." That alone made the trip worthwhile.

After that year, I made numerous trips to New York and she only joined me once more. That was the year that I took my entire staff of five people and flew them to New York for the Photo Expo. Not wanting to be left out, Jenny joined us, and with someone besides me to share it with, she had fun.

We'd only take one more major trip together after that, and she had to be forced into it. I had a shoot scheduled on New Years Eve in Fresno, California, and none of my staff wanted to be away on the biggest party night of the year. I even offered to add three days in San Francisco to the end of the trip, but amidst the staff's whining that they couldn't cancel their plans, Jenny was left with no choice. I needed an assistant, and she'd have to go. Of course we had a ball in San Francisco, exploring the shops and restaurants of the waterfront. We crossed the Golden Gate Bridge to Sausalito in a heavy fog, and found a charming restaurant on the San

Francisco Bay with huge windows facing the foggy waters. As we drank our wine, the fog lifted suddenly, giving us a stunning view across the bay of the brightly lit city. Jenny seemed to enjoy herself, but she insisted her traveling days were done.

But her days of wanting things were just picking up speed. We were both enjoying the lake house, but the only boat we ever took out was the small runabout. The houseboat sat at the dock, unused since we'd moved out of it. Other lake house owners had warned us that when you moved onto the lake you quit using your boats, but we weren't dock potatoes like them, that would never happen to us. But it did. There were just things to do, chores and projects, and our boating time only seemed to happen when we had visitors. So when Jenny started talking about selling the houseboat and buying something easier to maneuver, it sounded reasonable. I should have known the bait and switch was starting again. We talked about a small cruiser with a cuddy cabin, and not spending more than we got from selling the houseboat. The shopping started by visiting all of the marinas on Lake Hartwell and walking the docks looking at For Sales signs for just the right one. After weeks of looking unsuccessfully, we made the trip towards Atlanta to walk the huge Holiday Marina on Lake Lanier, where we had found our last houseboat.

None of the listings we had seen in the local boat sales flyers looked promising, but I knew I was in trouble when Jenny spotted a pristine 30 foot Bayliner Cabin Cruiser with a for sale sign in the back window. We stepped aboard, and while she gushed about how perfect it was, I looked at the sales information. It was $30,000! Substantially beyond our budget, and a lot more boat than we needed for evening cruises off of our dock on the lake. But she wanted it. And just like the four houseboats before it, the pressure didn't let up until she got it. A few weeks later the papers were signed, and the truck carrying our new toy met us at the ramp near Portman Marina. Jenny's need for things just kept growing, with bigger and bigger price tags every time.

The story was always the same, "I'm just not happy" she'd say. "But this will make me really happy!" And for a while it did. I was enjoying my work, studio, travel, home and sports car, and I just wanted her to share some of the happiness I felt. I still hadn't realized that I could never fill that great pit of need inside her by buying her the things she thought would bring happiness.

I didn't see it at the time, but her sense of entitlement was being stoked by a new set of friends. Our neighbors Josh and Maria had made a tidy sum by building lake homes, living in them a short while, and selling them for a large profit. He contracted them himself and did a lot of the work, so it was easy to make a profit in those days of real estate riches. His latest house two doors down from us was a 6,000 square foot home for the two of them, with an 800 square foot craft room with a 25 foot ceiling for Maria's stamp art projects. I felt like Jenny was living in luxury in our lakefront log home, but compared to Maria she felt like a poor relation. Another friend lived on a farm and raised dogs and show horses while her husband worked. Both of her friends drove new

Chevy Tahoes, and Jenny decided she had to have one as well. I told her a new $40,000. car was out of the question, and after a few weeks of pouting, she decided she "could live with a used one if I have to." She started shopping, and $26,000. later she had a used black Tahoe, same color as her friends. I didn't know then what her desire to "Keep up with the Neighbors" would lead to.

Part of the reason I kept giving in to Jenny's endless shopping was that things were going so well with my photography business. The light painting projects for Mount Vernon Mills and Michelin had been huge financial and critical successes. Now I was starting to dabble in digital photography. It was early 1998, well before the dawn of the digital age in photography, when I was thrust into the new technology. I was scheduled to do a three day hospital shoot for a TV commercial the following week, and was at a luncheon with Geno, an art director from the same agency. He and I were talking about the future of digital photography, and I mentioned that it might be a good way to shoot the presentation slides for the upcoming Addy Awards, the local edition of the national Advertising Federation contest for the best work in the field.

Next thing I know, Greg, the art director for the hospital TV shoot calls and says "Hey, Geno says that you're thinking about shooting the hospital project on digital."

"That's not exactly what I said", I told him.

But he was excited about the prospect, and after a short conversation I agreed. I've always been willing to learn on the job, but this was a little extreme. I did some quick research and found that I could purchase a Fuji one megapixel camera, with a built in zoom lens but no built in monitor for $3,000. I ordered the camera for overnight shipping, and had two days to learn how to use it before the shoot on Monday at a hospital almost 200 miles away. The remote monitor and back up memory card were shipped directly to the hospital.

The only reason I'd said the tiny one megapixel resolution would work for this project was because it wasn't for print use. The TV commercial would feature the still shots as quick popups on the screen, like a fast moving slide show. It was a challenge using such raw technology on short notice, but the three days went great, with only one hitch. That was when I was shooting scenes in the Emergency Room of two ER docs at work.

The doctors kept ending up across the table from each other, and when we got a break in the action I asked them "The next thing that comes in, if it's not a problem, could I get you two on the same side of the table?" They said that was fine, and we waited to see what would come in the door. We'd been listening on the emergency channels as they had picked up an older gentlemen at his home who wasn't feeling well. He'd walked himself to the ambulance, and no one seemed too concerned. Ten minutes out from the hospital, his heart stopped. They called a code, turned on the siren and started CPR, racing towards the hospital. When they arrived, the gurney came rushing through the door with a female EMT sitting astride the patient, pumping his chest as she tried to save his life. They hurriedly slid the patient onto the ER trauma table, and the staff surrounded him as they started shocking him with the paddles, starting IV's and working to revive him.

We started to back out of the room, but the staff head said "shoot it, shoot it!" so I stayed.

I was a little taken aback when one of the doctors lifted his head and asked me "Do you need us both on this side of the table?"

I told him "Don't worry about me, do what you need to!" and continued to shoot pictures of the dramatic scene.

After 20 minutes of futile effort, they all backed away from the table, the doctor said "Call it," and they looked at the clock to record the time of death. Everyone left the room, and the now deceased patient lay on the gurney, one arm dangling, the floor covered with the debris of the teams effort to save him. It was a stressful moment, and my assistant Amy, who was on her first hospital shoot, was in tears.

She said "I'm so upset, can I go outside for a cigarette?"

I told her, "I may join you, and I don't even smoke!"

It was an exciting and nerve wracking introduction to shooting digitally, but it would be four more years before the digital revolution swept over us completely.

Chapter Nineteen

Tuesday, November 23rd

After getting an early start out of Vero Beach, at mid-morning we made a quick stop at the Stuart Marina to pick up Rick's wife, Dellor. She'd be riding with us for the last two days of the trip, and I knew we'd both be glad of the female company after 12 days of being bachelors on this trip. There was no time for relaxing in Stuart and we were quickly back out into the St. Lucie River, headed for the crossing of Lake Okeechobee. Getting across the lake would take us more than a day, as there was 154 miles to travel between the five locks, and we also had to pass under three swing bridges, two drawbridges and a railroad lift bridge. There was no way to know for sure just how long it would take, and time was dwindling. There was a little more than two days until Thanksgiving, and I had promised I'd be home by then.

Crossing the lake was a real change from the nautical

experience of traveling the Intra Coastal Waterway down the east coast from Maryland to Florida. The largest freshwater lake in the state, Okeechobee is a native American name meaning Big Water, and while it covers 730 square miles, its average depth is only nine feet. It was important that we keep the Gibbous in the channels and not wander outside the lines to the muddy shallows, or we could quickly become mired in the muck. Once we got to the open body of the lake, the depths were more forgiving, and we only had to follow a compass course between the posted day marks. Fortunately it wasn't too windy, as the water can get pretty rough on the open lake. The Gibbous made it's way through the St. Lucie Lock, and under the swing bridge near Indiantown when we suddenly felt a large bump under the hull, and Rick quickly throttled back the engines, fearing we'd hit a floating log. Timber in the water can wait nearly invisible just below the surface, and has holed many an unsuspecting boat. We looked around us, and Captain Rick was surprised that what we had hit was not a log, but a giant carp. It was floating next to us, it's head torn off by one of our props. He used a pole to lift it out of the water, and it must have weighed 25 pounds even without its head. Fish running into the props was a rare occurrence, but that unlucky carp must have been napping as we came through the channel.

  We continued along unscathed, arriving at the Port Mayaca Lock shortly after our carp encounter. That was the last delay before entering the Big O, as the lake is known locally, and we were relieved that we locked through quickly. It was already afternoon, and we needed to make it to the locks on the other side of the lake before dark. Having Rick's wife Dellor aboard was a big help as we passed through the locks where line handling can get tricky, passing lines front and rear to the line handlers up on the lock walls, and dealing with as much as eight feet of depth change as you are raised or lowered to the new water level. When there are other boats in the locks with you, it can become a challenge to handle the lines front and rear with just two people, and the Gibbous is a heavy boat at more than 40,000 pounds, making it tough to hold in place.

As we made our way into the dark waters of the lake, it was calm, unlike its history. In 1926 the Great Miami Hurricane crossed over the lake, killing 300 people. Two years later in 1928, the Okeechobee Hurricane hit the lake, killing over 2,500. people. In both cases the deaths were caused by the storm surge flooding over the six foot dike that circled the lake. After those catastrophes, the US Army Corps of Engineers designed a plan for the construction of channels, locks and levees to prevent future destruction to the area. The Okeechobee Waterway was opened by President Herbert Hoover in 1937, and it has withstood the storms ever since.

We made our way slowly through the rest of the dark and quiet waters of Lake Okeechobee, skirting the edge of the lake as we headed for the Moore Haven Lock that would take us out of the lake's basin. The coffee colored water was beautiful, reflecting the bright colors of the surrounding trees into swirling patterns as our passing wake twirled the smooth surface. Arriving at Moore Haven, we made our way slowly through the lock, the gates closing behind us and the water rushing in like a filling bathtub as we were raised to the level of the water beyond.

We passed through the Ortona Lock and the Labelle Lock as the evening approached, but the sky darkened and a heavy fog rolled in, slowing our progress to a crawl. The original plan had been to make the trip from Maryland to Sarasota in 10 days, but our delayed departure from Oxford added one day, and the time waiting for bridge openings, lock openings and the many no wake zones had slowed us down a lot more. Not that it had slowed down Good Time Charlie. To him a no wake zone seemed like a challenge. But the bottom line was that we were nearing our destination, and it looked like I'd make my return to Greenville for Thanksgiving dinner as planned. The nearness of our destination made things more relaxed, and as we finally approached the end of our lake crossing in the twilight, we decided to anchor for the evening. Tomorrow would be the last day of the 1,300 mile trip, and we wanted to make it a good one. We'd made 146 miles in the calm waters of Lake Okeechobee that day, 1,141 total for the trip.

We sat on the foggy deck in the quiet evening, and Rick and Dellor wanted to hear the rest of my story, so over a couple of beers, I told them. They'd seen first hand my love of boats, and were surprised to hear that I no longer lived in the lake house of my dreams. All of the boats were gone except for a small 15 foot Hobie Jet which I trailered to the lake. It was hard to explain how it had all come about, and as I told them it seemed strange to me as well. Once again I'd tried to make Jenny happy.

In 1998, business was booming, and I was loving my work more than ever. Jenny had pretty much quit coming to work, and my staff had grown to six people, George and Vanessa, the associates who did their own photography projects, Amy, a full time assistant, a studio manager and a part time bookkeeper. There was also Amanda, who started as an intern in high school, and worked for us doing whatever she could help with during her college years at Furman. When Jenny and I asked her in her senior year about what she planned to do after graduation, she answered "Work for you guys!" Now, we had no idea that we were Amanda's career track, but I had always tried to be an encouraging boss, giving people opportunities I felt I'd had to fight to earn. The solution that developed over the next few weeks seemed to fit right in. We'd open a photography gallery in the studio, and let Amanda run it.

With three photographers, there had been a lot more work in the studio, and the building had shown signs of its age in the ten years I had owned it. We battled a leaky roof, storage of equipment, which took up much of the open space on the studio shooting floor, and I was sick of sharing an office with two other people. It seemed like a good time to expand, and a renovation would open up the building perfectly for a gallery. I refinanced the studio, finally getting rid of the Small Business Administration loan that had been a pain to get, and getting away from the local bank that had made the whole process so difficult. With the additional money I put a new membrane roof on the studio that finally ended the leaks, added a high ceilinged storage room off the rear of the studio which also allowed access to a deck overlooking the creek in the back, and put a nice office for myself on the balcony. My new office had a French door opening over the shooting floor, so I could make photos from that angle if necessary, but the staff seemed to believe it's real purpose was for keeping an eye on their activities. Being able to close my door and make phone calls was a luxury I'd waited a long time to have.

The next project was converting our lobby and studio to also work as a gallery. It had always been a great place to display images, so the main issue became installing a light grid to evenly illuminate the works. With that complete, the gallery just needed a name. The studio was located at 307 Townes Street, and we settled on DownTownes as the name of the new venture. Soon the gallery was filled with photographs from artists around the region, with opening nights bringing in as many as 300 people. It never made a profit, but helped to promote the studio and to introduce fine art photography to a new group of fans. And it gave Amanda a job.

We also began another long desired project, to find a way to control the light from the 12 sided dome in the ceiling. Steve, the studio manager, had a philosophy degree that didn't do much for running the business side of things. However, he turned out to be a creative whiz and his talents were invaluable during the renovation. He and George, one of the associate photographers, had worked together to kick around ways to control the light from the dome. Everything from rolling motorized shades to rotating irises was considered, but I knew the budget limitations we had, and wanted something that would be attractive as well as practical.

We finally settled on 12 pie shaped panels which would open like the petals of a flower, and would be raised from the closed position by a rotating spindle in the middle of the dome. I put Steve to work on a model, and he came back a couple of days later to show me the results. The 12 panels of the model had strings to pull them open, and the effect looked just right. I asked Steve if it was made to scale, and it was not. Feeling that the concept needed to be proven before we started building it, I sent him back to the drawing board for a scale model. When he brought it to me, my fears were confirmed. The height of the dome shaft didn't allow the panels to open fully when they were pulled from the center. Steve said "Let me think about it and see what I can do", and went back to the drawing board again.

When he came back the next time, the concept was amazing. He had drawn a system of cables that would be behind the dome walls, above the ceiling, and which would pull the 12 panels fully open. They would be controlled by a commercial garage door opener. The panels opened in 12 separate directions, and yet they were pulled from one source. This was achieved by a Rube Goldberg like series of pulleys around the outside of the dome. A panel next to the opener would pull straight back. One on the opposite side would pass through six pulleys to achieve the same effect. It was simple but brilliant. We purchased the materials, rented a 30 foot scaffold, and began the painting of the dome. It would have the sun painted on the pie shaped panels, which would open into a cloudscape painted on the dome's shaft, and a night sky with a star field on the top. Watching it come together was fascinating, and the first time Steve pulled the cable harness by hand and we watched to dome open, everyone burst out laughing. It looked like something from a James Bond movie.

It was truly amazing.

The last part of the project had long been a thorn in my side. There was an 800 square foot, falling down old shack that was right next to my beautiful studio. It was only 15 feet away, boarded up, and I had been trying to buy it from a group of six heirs for the past ten years. It's tough enough buying real estate from someone who doesn't want to sell, but getting that many heirs involved had made it impossible. It had been a tiny neighborhood grocery in the 1940's, and the families' memories made them reluctant to part with it. Now I had finally bought it, and was including it's renovation in my studio updating project.

The building was in terrible shape. There was a huge hole in the floor where crack heads had broken in from underneath to see if there was anything worth carting off, and all of the wiring and plumbing would have to be replaced. There was no heat and air, and it had a metal roof that leaked. The street side windows were barred and boarded up. The front corner wall was lower than the rest, and I chalked it up to the collapsed foundation on that spot. When we took the inside paneling off, it turned out that termites had eaten the bottom eight inches of every stud, and they were hanging, supported only by the outer siding. It was a big project.

After finishing the dome project, Steve went to work next door. He and I replaced the large front windows with glass block, giving it light, privacy and security on the busy street. The contractors did the bulk of the other work, but Steve's touches added the flair. We saved the tin ceiling in the front room, put a ribbed glass windowed door in the half bath, and Steve painted the front door. The front wall was faced with a tan brick, and I wanted it to match the studio, with it's multicolored red brick theme. Steve actually painted all of the bricks individually to make it match. The response from the neighborhood was wildly enthusiastic, as we'd turned an eyesore into an attractive cottage. With a full bath, bedroom, kitchen and half bath off the living room, we'd made a cozy place to stay when I had an early shoot or flight in Greenville.

I was pretty burned out on projects by the time all of this was complete, but Jenny was ready to start a bigger one. One night sitting on the side porch of my dream home on the lake, I was drinking a beer while she smoked, and she dropped her latest bomb.

"You know, I've always wanted a farm." She wanted a lot of things, so I wasn't initially concerned. Then she added "You know, prices for lake homes are sky high right now. We could sell this place, make a fortune and buy a farm!" I almost choked on my beer.

"Are you nuts?" I asked. "This is supposed to be our home to live in for 20 years, to retire from. We've only been here four years!" I told her to forget it, but she added a sweetener.

"Gee, with the money we made selling this house, we could pay off our debts, buy a little farm house to fix up, live smaller."

She knew I was tired of the large debt we carried and the work it took to support it all. I spent a lot of time juggling things to keep it all afloat. I still wasn't convinced, and I loved our house on the lake. We weren't using the cabin cruiser much more than we'd used the houseboat after moving into the home, but I still loved the whole lifestyle. This just seemed too hard to give up.

But of course, I underestimated Jenny's ability to sell me on the idea. She worked constantly over the next few weeks to convince me that we'd make a killing, even talking to a Realtor to back up her idea. I finally gave in, with one condition.

I told her "If we can sell this house for enough to pay off our debts, find a small fixer upper farmhouse, and live smaller so that I don't have to work so hard supporting it all, then I'll do it." Jenny enthusiastically agreed to the conditions, and we set off on the farm debacle.

We placed our lake home with a Realtor, and Jenny started her search for the farm of her dreams. We quickly found that the idea of a rustic farm on 25 acres for sale at a reasonable price was a fantasy. I had set the budget at under $200,000., and if we stuck to it, we'd have 20 acres with a shack or a mobile home on it. I asked Jenny to lower the acreage amount she wanted, and as we drove every back road imaginable looking for undiscovered gems, she was getting more and more discouraged.

She had worked with the Realtor to show me houses without acreage that she knew neither of us would like, and when I said they wouldn't do, her reply was "Well, it's what we can afford."

I could feel the pressure mounting as we scoured the real estate ads with no luck. Then she spotted Timm's Mill.

It was a hundred year old farmhouse on 48 acres with a barn and a pool, and it was for sale for half a million dollars. Jenny said she wanted to go look, and I told her that it was a waste of time.

"That's more than double our budget, I couldn't buy that for you if I wanted to!"

"Oh I know," she replied. "I just want to see it, and the Realtor has been wanting to see it too. It's just a fun excursion." I had misgivings, but she assured me she knew it was way out of reach for us, and that she was just curious to see it. We drove up to the house at the end of the long gravel driveway, and as the three of us got out, I knew I was in trouble.

"It's beautiful!" Jenny gushed as we walked into the country kitchen. The house had been remodeled in the 1970's, and looked like it. The kitchen had Harvest Gold appliances, and the hall stairs were covered with green shag carpet. The house had potential as a project, but not at $500,000. I thought the dated interior would turn Jenny off, but I was wrong again.

As we left after the tour, she said "It's perfect!" I reminded her of our financial limitations, but when she wanted something, it was my job to figure out how.

She spent the next three weeks, crying, cajoling, pleading, scheming, doing everything she could to talk me into it. Finally, I gave in. I told her that maybe we could split off some of the land, and build houses on them to make it affordable. I spoke to my neighbor the homebuilder, and he thought I'd lost my mind. After a few weeks of trying to think of ways to make it work, the Realtor called.

"There's an offer on the lake house, and it's a good one" she said.

With a few days of back and forth, the lake house was under contract, and we raced over to Timm's Mill to see if the owners were interested in any of our ideas. When we arrived, the For Sale signs lay in a pile by the mailbox. We frantically called the listing agent, who told us it was off the market. The owners had been trying to sell for two years, and they were tired of the hassle of showings. They were staying put. We asked the Realtor to tell them of our situation and reconsider, but they didn't want to talk to us. Jenny's Timm's Mill dream was dead.

Of course, privately I heaved a big sigh of relief. I knew that Timm's Mill could have brought financial disaster, because at more than double our budget, there was no way that any of my schemes to make it work could have actually made it affordable.

Jenny was bitterly disappointed, but we resumed our search for a farm. Having seen pretty much every possibility in a 40 mile radius, we turned to the idea of buying land and building the farm of her dreams.

We ended up finding nine and a half acres just a half mile from Timm's Mill, spent more than a third of our agreed on budget to purchase it, and started planning the house.

I didn't know it would be the path to ruin for us.

Chapter Twenty

Wednesday, November 24th

We awoke early, and by 8 a.m. we were underway in a heavy fog. It was hard to spot the channel markers in the pea soup, and we continued to be surprised when other boats sped by us, undeterred by the lack of visibility. They must have had more faith in GPS and radar than we did. After the long trek we'd made from Maryland over the last thirteen days, we were ready to get to the dock at Sarasota, but we wanted to get there in one piece.

The W.P. Franklin lock was the final one of our journey, and it was one I wanted to remember. Before this trip started, I had never been through a lock on a waterway, and now I'd been through so many I'd lost count. There were still a few bridge openings ahead of us, and I'd enjoyed them as well. Spending many family vacations in Florida as a child, I'd loved waiting in the back seat of the family VW, watching the bridges rise in front

Keeping Us Afloat

of us. I craned my neck for a view of the boats going by, wishing I was aboard. Now I had been on my own waterborne adventure, and I wasn't ready for it to end. I'd seen drawbridges, lift bridges, swing bridges that I'd never known existed, and a couple of ferries along this trip, and was fascinated by every one. The numerous tall highway bridges under construction that we had seen as we traveled down the ICW told me that many of those steel relics of the past would be gone in a few short years.

Now we were heading into the Gulf Coast side of the Intra Coastal Waterway for the final day of my cruise of a lifetime. With less than a hundred miles left in our 1,300 mile voyage, the sky cleared and we relaxed and enjoyed the beautiful sunny weather that contrasted wildly with the morning's heavy fog.

We were greeted on our passage into the Western side of the ICW by a pod of dolphins, leaping and weaving in our bow wake as we made our way towards Sarasota. Captain Rick drove the boat from the flybridge as Dellor and I stood on the deck, photographing the exuberance of the dolphins as they did a roller coaster like ride alongside the Waxing Gibbous.

With our more leisurely pace on this last day, Rick decided to stop at Cabbage Key for lunch. I was surprised, as we had not made a single meal stop during the previous 13 days of the trip. The only time we ate in a restaurant was when one was open where we docked for the night. Lunches had always been prepared and eaten while underway. Having Dellor along certainly made for a more relaxing day, and this stop was more evidence of that. We still had a long day's travel, but this was Captain Rick's home waters, and he knew how long it would take.

Cabbage Key is an unusual place, an island in the middle of Pine Island Sound at marker 60, near Sanibel and Captiva, that retains the charm of old Florida. It has a house that was built in the 1930's, when the island was first bought by Alan and Gratia Rinehart for $2,500. to be their winter estate. Constructed high on an Indian shell mound, Cabbage Key is one of the highest points in this area of Florida at 38 feet above sea level. Between 1944 and 1969 Larry and Jan Stults built additional cottages to rent and converted the main house into a restaurant, which has become famous over the last half century, with its Dollar Bar featuring thousands of dollar bills attached to the walls and ceilings by its numerous patrons, the bills adorned with handwritten notes. Current owners Rob and Phyllis Wells have lived on the island for the past 35 years, maintaining its old Florida style and charm.

The island is only accessible by boat, and as our Grand Banks neared the dock, Terry the dockmaster came to help tie us up to the pilings. The "Shower with a Friend" sign on the boathouse wall made me laugh, but with water a precious commodity on these isolated islands in the 30's and 40's, it may not have always been intended to be funny. We were a little early for lunch, and spent some time exploring the island, climbing the old wooden water tower and taking a few nice photos of Rick and Dellor together in the rustic tropical setting. After a lunch of Cabbage Key's famous cheeseburgers, we cast off from the dock, heading north now after nearly two weeks of pushing south. The last day of the trip was a quiet cruise as we passed numerous Manatee Zones, where we had to slow to a crawl to avoid the gentle sea cows which swim just under the surface.

The day seemed to fly by, and it was not yet sunset when we cleared the last bridge and made our way into the Gibbous' berth at Marina Jacks in Sarasota. It would be docked there for the next month as it underwent a full renovation before being moved to the Chitwood Charters rental fleet at the Sarasota Hyatt docks. I was spending the night at Rick and Dellors home before flying back to Greenville on Thanksgiving Day, sleeping in a real bed instead of my sleeping bag on the forward berth. It seemed odd that this adventure of a lifetime was coming to a quiet close.

The calm cruising waters had given me plenty of time to share the last of my saga of Jenny, houses and photography with my new friends. They wanted to hear what became of Jenny's farm dream, and the story was a wild one. The year had started with a fun shoot for Agfa, traveling with my assistant George to Montreal, Quebec to do a photo shoot at a hospital there. The CEO of the hospital was one of the subjects, and he didn't understand why I had flown thousands of miles to take his picture, when there were certainly many local photographers. He spoke only a little English, and my high school French was beyond rusty, but I tried to explain that there was a set of photos from different locations around the country, and that they all needed to have the same look, the same quality of light.

The CEO said with his heavy accent, "Oh, I get it, you are the artiste!"

We laughed, and for the rest of the trip George was calling me "The artist formerly known as David", a joking play on the musician Prince's experiment with a symbol in place of his name. George and I had some free time in Montreal before flying out the next morning, and spent the afternoon hiking in knee deep snow atop Mount Royal, the peak for which the city is named. Work was still an adventure for me, and sometimes a welcome break from dealing with Jenny's needs for grander things.

The farm was turning out to be the ultimate example of her wild schemes.

After we'd purchased the land, the planning had started for the house that we would build. The log home had been a tidy 2,000 square feet with a large unfinished basement, and I was thinking a smaller house would be the way to go, since we'd spent so much of our budget on the land. Jenny had a different idea. She felt that having been denied what she really wanted with the loss of the Timm's Mill dream, that she should have it made up to her with this home. I resisted, but before I knew it we had blueprints for a 2,500 square foot farm house with front and rear bay windows, a detached garage, wrap around porch, 25 foot cathedral ceilings showing off the soaring fireplace, and a heated pool.

And somehow, I was supposed to make it all happen.

The log home builder and I had parted on good terms, and in

spite of all the problems with that construction, he had made everything right in the end. So I made my biggest mistake of the project and hired him to build our latest dream home. What I didn't realize at the time was how little Gary would be involved in the building of this house. He had a new partner, Red, whose background was in building apartments, and he would be the on site supervisor. That quickly became a disaster. Red didn't like me, and didn't want to be told how to build the house. He was used to cost savings over custom design, and would pretend to go along with me only to ignore my requests and do it however he felt like it.

It started with the foundation. After months of delay, Red showed up one day with a rented BobCat and scraped some dirt away for the foundation. I'd been told that an excavation crew was being hired, but Red decided to save money and do it himself. I had specified that I wanted the house low to the ground, with no more than three steps at the front, and a direct doorway to the pool in the back, with no steps. The house was situated on a very slight rise, and that should have been easy to accomplish. I knew that the small excavation Red had done wouldn't provide for a crawl space that low to the ground, and I called the office and questioned him.

"Don't worry, we know what you want, and we know what we're doing" was the answer he gave. Then the batter boards went up, where they place boards along the foundation layout with strings to indicate where the concrete blocks go for the foundation. The boards on the front of the foundation were eight feet in the air!

I called the builder's office very agitated, and was told again by Red "Don't worry, we know what you want, and we know what we're doing, it will be how you want it."

He claimed the boards were just for guidance, and not indicative of how high the foundation would be. Then they started the block work, and the foundation quickly climbed to over seven feet tall in the front of the house, and four feet tall in the back. I decided it was time for action, and sent a fax to the builder Gary and to Red, telling them of my concerns. How would the house be low to the ground with a seven foot foundation!? The response was the same.

"Don't worry, we know what you want, and we know what we're doing." I should have called the whole project to a halt right then, but Jenny and I were frustrated with the delays we'd had, and I didn't want to lose the summer building season, so we let it go.

It seemed that every construction milestone brought a new error, and this time I wasn't living on the building site to catch them. After the framing of the house was completed, the carpenters started on the roof. I visited one evening to find that the entire 12 section roof had been framed, and I was appalled. The Donald Gardner designed house is drawn with two foot deep roof overhangs, and I'd seen many photos of completed homes that seemed to be less impressive than their drawings. I eventually noticed that it was because builders were building smaller roof overhangs than Gardner's team had drawn, losing the deep shadows that they created to give drama to the facade. When the contract for my home was written, the builder had specified eight inch overhangs, and I'd had him go back and change it to the correct two foot overhangs as drawn. We all initialed the change, but no one bothered to tell Red. They had built the entire roof of our house with eight inch overhangs. I was very upset, and called Gary the builder to complain, and to remind him of that initialed correction to the contract. He remembered, but was distraught.

"David, do you know what it will cost me to tear that whole roof off and start over!?"

He estimated about $15,000. between the labor and wasted materials, and left it to me to find a solution. What I came up with was a compromise at best. The facade's visual shadowing from the deeper overhangs came primarily from where the roof ends protruded from the peaks, not from where the roof sloped down to the edge. So I had the builder go back and extend all of the roof ends to their full two foot depth, something that was impossible where the slanted sections descended. It was better than nothing, and it helped the visual appeal of the house. Gary heaved a sigh of relief that I didn't make him tear the roof off.

Meanwhile, I was working overtime on ways to make the house affordable. I decided to paint the inside of the house myself, saving $6,000. toward Jenny's pool. I also made a deal with the pool company to photograph some of their exotic pool installations in trade for a $3,000. discount on our pool. Those two things covered about half the cost. So I spent my weekends putting 65 gallons of paint onto the walls and ceilings, standing on a ladder atop a scaffold to do the 25 foot high peaks in the great room.

During the summer weeks I worked in between photo shoots to first build a fence around five acres, digging posts for a wooden fence on one side and wire fence on the other three. Then I started the 36x36 foot four stall barn with its 18 foot high roof peak down the center aisle. I bought a truckload of rough sawn pine from the sawmill in Pickens 20 miles away, and hauled it in our recently purchased horse trailer to the building site. It overloaded the trailer so badly that it fishtailed wildly at anything over 30 miles an hour, so I made the 20 mile trip at a crawl. Setting the 24 foot long poles for the center of the barn into their holes in the ground was accomplished by standing atop 16 feet of scaffolding and lifting the poles with a rope while a helper on the ground guided the base into the hole. I'd designed the barn myself, modifying a stock pole barn drawing to create the classic Midwestern barn look we desired, and nailed all of the roof trusses into place from the scaffold with one hand while holding them in place with the other. By the end of the summer I was exhausted. My hands were raw from the rough wood, which shredded leather gloves, and my back was sore from constantly working on building and painting with my arms up in the air.

Meanwhile Jenny was doing, well ...., nothing.

She had agreed to paint the trim around the windows and doors, but hadn't made much progress. She loved to visit the building site and give tours to friends and neighbors, but she wasn't doing anything constructive. We were living in the small apartment next door to the studio in the synagogue downtown, but she wasn't even coming to work there. She read books, watched TV, played with the dogs and cats, and shopped. It was frustrating to watch as I slaved on building her dream house. One night we were at a department store, and she found a wood and metal dining room set with a baker's rack that she thought would look perfect in our new home's dining room. It was attractive, but I didn't think we needed to spend the $5,000. cost when we were struggling to finish the house. She enticed me to humor her by making me promises about boosting our love life in return for the new set, but it was a promise she never kept. Jenny was the queen of credit cards, and we left the store as owners of new furniture.

In my spare time, we were taking riding lessons. A big part of Jenny's farm dream was owning horses, so we were taking lessons just around the corner from the farm construction. She was a nervous rider, and horses are very sensitive to that. Signs of anxiety put them into flight mode, fearing attack by wild predators, and Jenny was full of anxiety. She was confined to riding an older horse in the round pen, while I was going on longer rides in the pastures, learning to trot, canter and gallop. We got very bad advice from our trainer, who had a two year old horse he wanted to sell me. All of the conventional wisdom was that novice riders were better off with older, well trained horses, but we trusted him, and I bought Chase, a raw red gelding Quarter Horse.

Jenny bought a three year old Quarter Horse mare from a friend who trained horses, at more than double the cost of my purchase. I learned to ride, and she learned to fall. She fell from her horse during training in the round pen, and cracked two ribs. That put an end to her riding for six months.

Construction on the house moved along briskly during the summer, with more and more irritations coming with it. I pulled in front of the house site one evening, and noticed something looked off about the front. The carpenters had built two dormers on the roof that day, and they had an elongated look, like a top hat instead of a bowler hat. I called and told the builder of the problem, and a short time later the visibly angry head carpenter came flying up the gravel drive in his pickup. He skidded to a stop, grabbed a ladder off the rack and slammed it against the roof.
He climbed to one of the dormers, ripped the measuring tape out against the side, and stopped.

A look of confusion replaced his anger and he said "I'll be damned." The dormers were a foot and a half too tall. It became one more thing done wrong, as the house I'd envisaged from the drawings turned out to not look quite right.

The next thing was the wrap around porches. Once again I'd been out on a photo shoot, trying to make enough money to keep this crazy project going, and when I made a trip to check the day's progress, I could not restrain my anger. The porches should have been level with the doors, and Red had dropped them to nearly a foot lower in an effort to convince me that the foundation wasn't as tall as I feared. The drop from the doorways was a shock, and I could imagine the potential for accidents. Once again Gary the builder begged me not to make him rip all of the porches off, and we ended up with small six inch steps at all five doors opening onto the porches. As it neared completion, the interior of the house was beautiful, although it was hard for me to look at the outside without being overwhelmed by all of the mistakes they had made. Gary had always been a custom builder, and by partnering with Red had thought he could be more competitive with Red's knowledge of economy building. But the two styles didn't mix well, and our house paid the price of his experiment. Gary eventually ended up as frustrated as I was with Red's corner cutting, and the two parted ways at the end of our project.

The last surprise came as we prepared to move in. Gary presented me with a bill for nearly $30,000. worth of cost overruns! I laughed at him, telling him that with all the mistakes they'd made on this house, he wasn't getting another dime. We both argued and threatened law suits for days, but he finally agreed to a much reduced overrun bill. Neither of us was happy, but it was over, the house was done.

Chapter Twenty-One
Journey's End

When I awoke Thanksgiving morning in the guest room of Captain Rick's Florida home, it seemed strange not to feel the rocking of the boat. My flight back to Greenville left in a few hours, heading back to the reality of work and the struggle to make my wife Jenny happy. This was the longest I'd been gone from my studio or from Jenny in our more than 25 years of marriage. I'd really enjoyed the break from the long work days my photography career entailed, but was looking forward to seeing Jenny. Being ever the romantic, I envisioned being welcomed with open arms on my arrival after such a long time away. I ate a quiet breakfast with Rick and his wife, as we were both finally talked out after two full weeks of sharing stories.

Rick drove me to the airport, and I thanked him again for the wonderful experience he'd shared with me traveling the Intra

Coastal Waterway. We promised to keep in touch, and I boarded the plane. The flight from Sarasota landed at the US Airways hub in Charlotte, NC after less than two hours in the air and I thought I was almost home. But it was foggy in Charlotte, and the flight was delayed. Finally, we boarded the plane, only to be told there was a problem with the landing gear and asked to deplane again. An hour went by, and a replacement aircraft arrived to pick us up. It was 2 p.m. when I landed at Greenville Spartanburg Airport, but my travel problems weren't over yet. With all of the plane changing, US Airways had lost my luggage. Flying may have been faster, but my trip on the ICW had been much more reliable and pleasant.

Instead of the expected welcoming arms of my wife, my Mom was at the airport to pick me up. I did get a big hug from Mom, who loved to travel as much as I do, and she couldn't wait to hear all about the trip. Seems like Jenny had some kind of bug, and didn't feel well enough to pick me up. Mom drove me to the apartment next to my studio and dropped me off. We still hadn't moved into the farmhouse, waiting as the finishing touches were applied. When I walked in the door, my hopes for an open armed welcome evaporated again.

"Hi. I thought you'd never get home", Jenny sniffed, a box of tissues next to her.

She didn't even get up from the couch to say hello. I know she was under the weather, but this was surely not the romantic welcome I'd imagined in my nights aboard the Waxing Gibbous.

She informed me that she hadn't cooked anything because she felt bad, and that I would be going out to lunch with my parents, sister and nephew. Jenny would be staying home. A buffet lunch at a restaurant on Thanksgiving Day just wasn't part of what I dreamed of for this day. I really wondered why I'd worried so much about making it back by Thanksgiving at all.

I wish I could say that Jenny got well, we moved into the farm and lived happily ever after, but that's not what happened. Probably the best day at the farm was the day we moved in, the punch list finally complete. Jenny drove me the next day to the nearby horse training facility, where I got on my horse Chase, and the trainer got on Jenny's horse Shadow. We rode them across the fields to our own pasture, and I put them in their stalls at our newly built barn. Even though she couldn't ride while recovering from her broken ribs, Jenny was as excited as I'd ever seen her, and I thought maybe it had all been worth it. The dream of the farm was finally a reality.

We'd stored our furniture in an air-conditioned indoor facility in nearby Anderson while we built the farmhouse, and when I went to retrieve it for the move to the new home I got a surprise. Termites had come through a crack in the floor and eaten into the frame of our oak futon. When I talked to the manager of the facility, she was appalled and apologetic, but told me that the company had a disclaimer that they were not responsible for any damage to contents of their storage units.

"I certainly think termites coming through the floor would be your responsibility" I replied. "It sure isn't my fault!"

The manager put me in touch with their Atlanta office, where I spoke with a VP. She gave me the same story, that their disclaimer released them of any liability.

The conversation became heated, and I told her "Would you like me to put a billboard next to your facility that says 'This building has termites, don't store your goods here'"? She hemmed and hawed for several minutes before caving and agreeing to pay for the damaged futon. When I emptied the building and handed the keys back to the manager the next week, she was amused.

"I heard from the VP at the Atlanta office that you spoke to" she said, "and she told me you threatened to put up a billboard saying we had termites!"

The VP had asked her 'Do you really think he'd do that?'"

The manager chuckled and said "I told her, you know, I think he just might!"

Back at work after the move, my photography business took off again, starting with shooting the BMW family of cars for a giant display in the nearby manufacturing plant. My staff, me and the art director drove the four shiny Z3's and two X5's up into the mountains, to an overlook we had selected previously. My truck full of lighting gear followed along behind, and we spent hours doing a group shot of the cars for the mural. After the shoot, we had a blast racing the cars back to BMW along the twisting mountain roads.

It was hard to believe I was getting paid for having this much fun.

The next adventure was a Michelin shoot. The art director had concepted three ads for their truck tire division that emphasized the gas mileage savings that Michelin Tires gave the drivers of the big rigs. The campaign was to show offbeat alternative ways to save gas, and the first two ads had been shot in Hollywood, using the special effects techniques available there. I was thrilled when the Art Director, Steve, asked me to quote the third ad. It showed an 18 wheeler on a curving road by the seashore, with a majestic sail atop the truck giving it a push towards better gas mileage as the sun set behind it. The only problem was that to make it affordable, it had to be shot on the East coast. The long curvy seaside road by the dunes in the drawing for the proposed ad is apparently common on the west coast, but doesn't exist on the East coast. I contacted location scouts in North Carolina, Georgia and Florida, trying to find what I needed. Most roads were not waterfront, and the ones that were had telephone poles, trees and all kinds of other issues that made them unworkable. The need for a sunset made it impossible.

After looking at unsuitable location snapshots from scouts throughout the three week scouting period, I was out of patience. The project was coming up fast, and I didn't have a place to shoot it. I packed a bag, got in my little Z3, put the top down and headed for Florida. In just over two days I drove 1,400 miles looking at beach fronts, from the East coast to the West coast to the panhandle of Florida, and came up with a plan. We'd shoot the beachfront at St. Joe Island, in the elbow of the panhandle, which had a great waterfront for the sunset image we needed. I'd found the perfect road farther North, curving through the dunes next to the water on Santa Rosa Island in the upper panhandle. The only problem was that St. Joe Island is a state park, and Santa Rosa Island is in a National Wildlife Preserve. At Santa Rosa you are not allowed to pull off the road even in an emergency for fear of disturbing nesting seabirds. Getting permission to park a big rig on that curving two lane road while we photographed the ad would be a challenge.

But then, challenges had never stopped me before. The Art Director loved my sample shots, and I started working the phones to get the needed permits for the shoot. We'd gotten a break when we found the perfect sail on a boat in Charleston harbor. We'd expected the $100,000. translucent carbon fiber sail specified for the ad might only be found in places like Newport, Rhode Island, where serious racers congregate. While awaiting approvals for the Florida portion of the shoot, the AD Steve and my crew headed to Charleston, where we'd chartered both the sail boat and a smaller chase boat which we would follow along in, photographing the sail in motion using a gyroscope to steady the camera. It was great fun, fighting the pitching of the waves, and directing the sailboat by walkie talkie to get the sun behind the sail as we cruised past it.

In just a few hours, we had that part of the ad in the can. Now came the hard part. Permits finally in hand, we made the long drive to the Florida panhandle, working a tight schedule for the two shots. We drove straight through to St. Joe Island, arriving in time to capture the sunset over the water. There was no road near the water, so we perched atop the dunes to catch the right angle. Then it was on to Santa Rosa the next morning to meet the park rangers and the big rig we had rented for the shoot. When we arrived at the park, the rangers were ready, and the truck was sitting at the Ranger station, waiting for us. The Michelin tires had been shipped to a dealer so they could be mounted on the truck, and they were on the correct side, but no one had thought to wash either the truck or the tires. It was a sight to see the three of us out there with spray cleaner and shop towels, spraying and wiping down the tires. We set up the camera and tripod as far off the road as we were allowed to go, being careful not to step on any grasses or plants. The rangers were watching, and I think even they were surprised we'd gotten permission for this shoot. The photography went beautifully, and afterwards we celebrated by parking at the public beach and running and jumping into the surf. At least at work, life was good.

Things weren't so good at home. Jenny was healed from her broken ribs, but was too nervous after her accident to get on her horse. She loved feeding and petting the horses, but riding didn't seem to be in her future. Horses need to be ridden or they become uncooperative, so she was inviting anyone who was willing to come ride her horse. I'd known my friends Charlie and Mona since college, and Mona had been dying to ride, so one Saturday I invited her over. When she arrived at the house we all said the usual pleasantries, but Jenny stayed indoors while Mona and I headed out to the barn. After saddling up, we started the rounds of the five acre pasture, giving the horses a small workout. When we stopped at the far corner, looking back at the barn and house, I couldn't help but sigh. "This was Jenny's dream, not mine. I so wish she could be here enjoying this." Mona was understanding. She knew it wasn't a comment on her company.

We finished the ride, then put up the horses and she drove home. The reaction from Jenny caught me by surprise.

"It looked like you were having a great time on MY horse with Mona!" she spat. I'd let Mona ride my horse, since Jenny's horse Shadow was often skittish.

"That couldn't be farther from the truth", I answered. Actually I was out there saying how much I wished you were there!"

She said "Oh, sure you were."

Things hadn't been going well between us, and jealousy was something I had always hated. Our sex life had frequently been difficult, with Jenny's moods making our romantic evenings totally unpredictable. There were many times I knew lovemaking was out of the question, but the hardest days were when she promised all day long that "Tonight's the night." I'd go around singing Rod Stewarts's song of the same name at the top of my lungs, only to be crushed when she said her usual "I just can't tonight" at the last possible minute. After putting up with a quarter century of that, I sure didn't feel I deserved her jealousy.

Jenny no longer came to work, but she found time to do a lot of socializing with friends in Anderson where we lived. There was Maria, the wife of the builder who was a neighbor in our lake neighborhood. She lived in huge and luxurious house on the lake, a lifestyle Jenny thought was very attractive. Then there was Donna, who lived on a ten acre farm and raised horses and show dogs. Her engineer husband had recently bought her a $10,000. horse. Lastly there was Gabrielle, the Frenchwoman who was a sculptor and horse trainer. She was divorced from a Brazilian financier, and lived on a 45 acre lakefront farm. These were the women who were Jenny's new role models. None of them worked at a job, and all of them lived a life of great comfort. One evening while at Gabrielle's for dinner, I spotted a framed photo of a castle on the kitchen wall. When I asked about it, I was floored by the response.

"Oh, that's Mama's chateau", she said. "It's where I grew up."

And Jenny was getting her ideas of what life should be from these women.

Don't get me wrong, I liked them just fine. But all three of them had the kind of money that we would never have, and Jenny wasn't going to live like them. She started to believe she deserved it though.

The first year at the farm brought with it the newness that Jenny always craved, but it didn't take long for her to become dissatisfied.

Keeping Us Afloat

Every time we drove past the 48 acre farm at Timm's Mill, she put her hand over her heart, sighed, and said "Ah, Timm's Mill, what might have been." This just drove a stake in my heart every time she said it. And with its nearness, we drove by the huge farm often. I'd worked myself into the ground to build a home I thought she wanted, and she was treating it like a consolation prize.

She'd added a Doberman to our menagerie, one more thing she'd "always wanted", and was wanting to spend money for obedience training, something she was perfectly capable of doing herself.

When I told her we couldn't afford it, she said "You're so MEAN".

Just as Jenny's desire for more and more things was growing, the financial pressure on me was increasing. She had busted the budget we'd agreed to on the house by nearly $100,000., and the payments were exorbitant. There were a lot of expenses with the new home, including a horse trailer to pull behind her Tahoe, and a used John Deere tractor and attached Bush Hog for cutting the pasture. I'd insisted on no grass at the lake house and had even sold the mower, and yet now I was spending 10 hours one day every month Bush Hogging the property. And the timing couldn't have been worse for these budget busters. The ad market for commercial photography suddenly declined, and I was struggling to stay afloat.

We met with an American Express financial adviser who I'd

known when he was a reporter, and he advised us to stay the course.

"You've been in business 15 years, and the work always comes back", he said. "Borrow the money to get through this downturn, and then you'll be on top and ready to work when it's over."

It seemed like good advice, and a lot more pleasant than laying off my staff, all of whom felt like family members to me. So we borrowed $50,000. against the farm, and I gave Jenny this caution before we signed the papers.

"If we go through the whole line of credit, and the economy still hasn't bounced back, we'll have to sell the farm."

She agreed, but seemed unconcerned. After all, I'd always made things happen, and she believed I would again. Every month, when the bills were paid at the studio and at home, I told her how much I'd drawn from the line of credit. She continued to want to spend money on clothes, furnishings, pets, dinners with her friends, and more.

She passed off my objections with "You're just being mean." One month I had a trip to Celebration, Florida, planned for a shoot for Agfa. Celebration was the town built by Disney near Orlando's Disney World, and I tried to entice Jenny along with a trip to the giant amusement park.

"You know I can't go, who would take care of the horses and the dogs?!" was her reply.

I was flying out of Greenville early in the morning, and was in the bed reading when Jenny came stumbling in the house, blood running down her face.

"What happened!" I asked.

She replied shakily "I went to water the horses in their stalls, and they wanted to go into the round pen. When I opened the gate they spooked and stampeded over me."

She didn't seem badly hurt, just scared, as anyone would be when a few thousand pounds of horseflesh runs over you. I bundled her into the Tahoe and drove to the emergency room in Greenville, where they made us wait for hours. After seven hours there, the doctors decided she had a mild concussion, and sent us home. She didn't even need stitches for the cut on her head. We got home at 7:30 a.m., just enough time for me to shower and make it to the airport. I asked if she would be OK alone, and offered to have my parents come look after her, but she said she was fine. It felt strange to be leaving her to go to Disney World and have fun, but she knew how badly we needed the work, and didn't want me to cancel the shoot either.

So I spent the next day touring Disney World with my assistant Amy, riding all of the rides in the rain. It was great, because the bad weather kept the crowds at home, and it felt like we had the park to ourselves. The next day was the shoot at Celebration Health, an adventure in itself. The administrators wanted the hospital to have something of the Disney feel to it, and had added touches like a video wall with a giant aquarium scene in the lobby. The radiology department was built to look like a boardwalk, with beach chairs for the waiting areas, beach scenes painted on the walls, the sounds of surf and seagulls playing in the background and even a scent generator putting the smell of coconut oil in the air. The CAT scanner was modified by the Disney set shop to look like a giant sandcastle. The head radiologist told me that one of the first patients, an elderly woman, was seen with tears running down her cheeks after they put her in the machine and looked through the observation window. The tech stopped the scan and rushed in to check on her, thinking she was frightened of the scanner.

"This reminds me of going to the beach as a child!" she said between sniffles. It was an incredible place, and a fun location to shoot.

When I got home to the farm after three days, Jenny had recovered from her trampling, but her emotions had not. She was terrified of the horses, and her nervousness translated into a danger message to them, making them agitated and jumpy. The horses that were such a big part of Jenny's dream of living on a farm seemed to become her personal cross to bear. I had only taken riding lessons to humor her, but the fact that I learned to ride passably well while she was too nervous to get up on her horse at all just made her resent me more. Jenny had always been irritated by my sunny outlook on life, and by the success that came my way. Not that she minded spending the money that came with it.

Even her parents had contributed to the problem. They had constantly nagged her to finish school, which just seemed to make it harder for her to achieve. When I graduated from college, and later opened a business that was successful, they just couldn't say enough nice things about me, while continuing to look down on their own daughter.

I told Jenny's mother more than once how much Jenny needed her approval, and her reply always started with "If she'd just go back and finish school..." I didn't need the emotional support, as I got plenty of it from my own super supportive parents. Jenny was desperate for the same approval from her folks, and could never get it. It just seemed to give her one more point of resentment towards me.

Things limped along with our relationship after that. I was getting less patient with her financial demands after all that we'd put into the house, and one night things came to a head. After a long day at work, I arrived home at 7 p.m. As I pulled into the driveway, Jenny walked out onto the back porch steps.

When I got out, camera bag on one shoulder and computer bag on the other, she said as I walked towards the house, "Oh good, now that you're home you can help me hang curtains."

I was exasperated, and said "Do you mind if I set this stuff down and sit for a minute first? I haven't even gotten in the house yet." Her reply was amazing.

She put her hands on her hips and snapped "I just get NO help around here!"

Now, being the person who had just finished painting the

entire house, fencing five acres and building a barn for her horses, I was pissed. Uncharacteristically for me, I blew up.

I told her "You know how much I've done to build this place, running the business at the same time without any help from you, and by God I deserve to sit down when I get home!"

She said again how mean I was, something that had become a theme for her in recent months.

When I left for work a few days later, I asked Jenny to call the plumber. There was a leak under a newly installed sink, and I wanted it fixed before too much time passed. She said she would, and I didn't think anymore about it. When I returned home that night and asked if she'd called the plumber, she blew up at me.

"NO, I didn't call the plumber! Do you know how much I had to do today? I had to go to the grocery, walk the dogs, feed the horses, skim the pool, when do think I'd have time to call the plumber?!"

I asked her why she had agreed to make the call that morning if she wasn't going to do it, but she didn't want to discuss it anymore.

This was part of a new tactic she'd developed. When you haven't done something you promised to do, go on the offensive when questioned. Make it appear that the other person should not have expected it from you in the first place. It wasn't that different from other things she'd done throughout our marriage, but I was having less and less patience with it. I'd always worked harder than she had during our 27 years together, but the incredible amount of work I'd done in the past year and a half to build her dream farm had burned me out. I just couldn't stand to hear her complaints while she contributed so little.

Jenny was becoming increasingly isolated from the studio and from our Greenville family and friends. When we'd lived on the lake, which was farther from Greenville than the farm, she still managed to occasionally come to work, and to come to Greenville for family dinners, socializing with friends, etc. Now she seldom left the farm. I got used to doing things alone in town, and grew very accustomed to the question "Where's Jenny?" I made excuses for her, but it was apparent to everyone that something was wrong. One event I'd always insisted she participate in was the annual advertising industry awards. The Addy Awards was a dinner and awards presentation, and my photography had received over 100 awards from the group during the past 15 years. It was important to me and to our business. Jenny had complained every time February came around that she hated it, but it was one of the very few things I insisted she do. But in the year of the farm, she said she was NOT going, and there was nothing that would change her mind. So I went with friends and spent the evening explaining my wife's absence.

As bad as things had gotten, I was still surprised when she suggested in April of 2000 that we separate.

Chapter Twenty-Two

When I set off on the trip down the ICW with Captain Rick aboard the Waxing Gibbous, I was on top of the world. As a busy and successful photographer traveling the US and abroad, I'd been married over a quarter century and I was building a dream home and farm for what I thought was my loving wife. It's kind of stunning how quickly things changed.

Jenny had thrown the divorce card out many times in the last decade, but it was always in the middle of a fight.

We'd be arguing, and she'd say "Why don't you just leave? You'd be better off without me!"

I always told her how hurtful that was, and I knew that she was using it as a weapon. This was different. She was in the barn with the horses, it was a beautiful spring day, and I thought things were as fine as they ever were.

When she turned to me as I walked in and said "I think maybe we should be apart for a while." I was shocked. It wasn't said in anger, but calmly, deliberately. When I asked her what she was saying, she didn't have a good answer. "We're just not getting along, we want different things. I just think we should be apart, see what happens." I protested that I loved her, and that splitting up was the last thing I wanted, but she was unmoved.

Over the next five months, I did everything I could think of to change her mind.

She had always said "We need counseling!" when she was mad at me, so I told her I'd find us a marriage counselor. But now that I was willing, she didn't want to go. After much cajoling, we went to our first counseling session together. The counselors initially thought we had some minor issues, because we seemed so easy together.

"Oh, you two just need a 'tuneup' for your marriage" was what they'd said.

It didn't take long to see how deep the divisions really were. I'd written many letters to Jenny during the days after she suggested we separate. She didn't like to have long conversations about our issues, and I found it easier to put my thoughts into writing, where I knew she couldn't remember things that I had never said, or cut me off without letting me finish. One long letter had many personal things about our sex life and how much more I wanted from it, and about how I wanted Jenny to be a part of things at work and with my family. She thought it was terribly negative, and threatened to show it to the counselors. When I agreed, the response wasn't what either of us expected.

When one of them read the letter, she looked up at both of us and said "There's just so much love in this letter!"

Jenny was fuming, and was soon calling the biweekly meetings "Bash Jenny" sessions. The problem was that I wanted to fix things between us, and she just wanted someone to tell me I was the one in the wrong.

During one session I suggested that we let go of the studio bookkeeper, and that Jenny come in two half days a week to do the books. That's eight hours a week. The counselor thought that was a wonderful idea.

"That would help your finances, and give Jenny a way to contribute. And you will spend more time together to boot. What a wonderful suggestion!"

Jenny didn't say much, but when we got to the car afterwards, she exploded. No way was she coming back to work! I asked why, when we needed the financial support, she couldn't work just eight hours a week?

"I just thought that at my age I would finally get some time to myself! Time to write, paint, garden, just some time for myself!" was her answer.

It was pretty hard to take, since she was not working at anything that I could see. I asked why it was fair for me to work so many hours and for her not to work at all.

She said "But you like your work!"

Jenny had always been difficult, but this was a new height of selfishness that was hard to understand. I'd spent so many years trying to make her dreams come true, to actually make her happy. I had to admit to myself that I'd failed.

One sign of my failure to make her happy was the farm itself. I asked her one evening during her usual wine and cigarette session on the back porch how she really felt about the farm.

"Whenever you go by Timm's Mill, you sigh and get all misty eyed about it", I said.

"So, can't a girl dream?" was her reply.

"The problem", I said, "is that it makes me feel like this farm, which looks like a palace to our friends with the house, barn and the pool, just seems like nothing more than a consolation prize to you."

"Yeah, so?" was her reply.

I was pretty stunned. I'd worked my tail off to build her a consolation prize. One that wasn't what she really wanted. Her lack of appreciation for all my efforts was appalling. Sometimes I think she just wanted to see how much she could hurt me, and that comment certainly did hurt.

She persisted in asking that I move out, and I finally offered to use an empty apartment we had next door to the studio during the week to give her space. She agreed that could help, but it became contentious.

One of our regular fights had been about my artwork.

I photograph nude figure studies, something Jenny had initially supported and even encouraged. They'd been exhibited at numerous museum shows and the state fair and had won a number of awards. One print was scheduled to be part of a group show at the Greenville Museum that fall. Jenny seldom complained about the work, and had even helped on one shoot after suggesting the subject matter, but she began feeling that they were "inappropriate" for display outside of a gallery setting. When I mentioned how excited I was about hanging my artwork in the new house when it was completed, she snapped at me.

"Absolutely not! I won't have those on MY walls. What would the neighbors think?"

I was extremely unhappy about this, but she wouldn't budge. I can't describe how resentful it made me to have my wife refuse to allow my artwork on the walls of the home I was building for her. I intended to rebel and at least hang some in my study at the house, but in the short time we lived there before she asked me to leave things were so contentious that it didn't seem worth the fight.

When I started moving a couple of things from storage to the empty apartment to begin using it, Jenny voiced no objection, even asking me to swap a portable TV for a console we had in storage so she could have the smaller one from the apartment to use in the bedroom at the house. I even began thinking maybe this living quarters compromise could head off the disaster that our marriage was becoming.

The day of one of our gallery openings, I had planned to stay the night there to avoid having to make the long drive home after drinking wine. I'd only spent a handful of nights there, but Jenny seemed to be in agreement that it was working out ok. I took the opportunity that day to hang some of my artwork in the apartment. I carried 18 framed prints over to the apartment from the studio next door, and had about 12 of them hanging with the help of an employee when Jenny walked in, saw them on the walls, and stormed out without a word. I could tell she was angry, but when I went next door to try and talk to her she wouldn't speak with me.

She only said "You've made your choice mister. I see that now, you've made your choice!"

She seemed to take the hanging of my artwork as an unacceptable statement of my independence. Her implication was also that I was setting up a bachelor pad to party with women. When I asked her if that was what she thought, she said no. I even asked her if she thought I was having an affair or something, but she said no, but that I couldn't be trusted. She didn't want to live with me, but she didn't want me to live anywhere else either. What a choice.

From the moment she had first suggested separation, it seemed to be all she wanted. After five months of trying to avoid it, the marriage counselors finally threw in the towel and suggested separation. I gave up and moved out. The timing was lousy. We'd rented the small apartment the week before to a massage therapist to use as her office. Jenny had encouraged it when the subject came up, and I thought that meant she was rethinking her idea of separation. Now I wonder if she wasn't just trying to limit my options. Do things exactly the way she wanted, which included buying her whatever she desired and not expecting her to come to work anymore, or be out in the cold with nowhere to turn. The large apartment in the lower level of the studio was under a long term lease, so that wasn't an option either.

    I spent the first two weeks of our separation sleeping on a couch in the middle of my studio, then moved the couch into my office for some privacy. After six weeks on that too short couch, I borrowed a bed from a friend and turned my office into an office/bedroom. The studio had a kitchen and half bath but no shower, and I worked out a deal with the massage therapist next door to use the shower every day before she arrived to work at 9 a.m. I felt conspicuous making my daily trips down the sidewalk to the building next door at 8 a.m. with towels and my shaving kit in hand, but at least it was free. My living quarters had not been comfortable or private, but with our difficult finances I didn't feel I could afford to rent anything else. On the weekends I went to the farm, trying to finish the trim painting, cutting the pastures, caring for the horses, and sleeping in the guest room. I was still trying to get Jenny to reconcile, but she was unmoved.

    Finances weren't getting any better either. Work was still off its normal pace, and the bills from the farm were bleeding me dry.

    Every month as I took money from the credit line to cover the shortages, I told Jenny "Here's what I'm taking, and here's how much is left in the credit line." When the month came that I told her there was only $2,000. left from the $50,000. credit line, I gave her the news I'd been dreading.

"We'll have to sell the farm."

She said little, but the next day made a rare trip into Greenville to the studio, where she parked herself at the bookkeepers desk, and spent hours going through all of the accounts and the income. When she was finished, she came into my office, shut the door and flopped down on the couch.

"Why didn't you tell me things were this bad?" she said. I'd been giving her a running account of the situation monthly, and didn't understand how she could be surprised.

I said "What part of 'We'll have to sell the house' was unclear?"

This, of course, did not make our relationship problems any better. But she could see the writing was on the wall, and we began making plans to sell the farm.

There was still trim painting and landscaping that needed to be completed, and my weekends were devoted to getting as much done as possible so that we could sell the house. One such weekend finally brought things to a head. When I'd left the Sunday before, Jenny and I talked about the things we still needed to finish to get the farm ready to sell. I told her that the riding mower for trimming the lawn around the house needed a belt replaced, and asked if she could take it to the dealer. We had a small trailer that hooked up behind her Tahoe, and she could just drive it up the ramp to load it. She agreed. We also planned on planting bushes and trees around the foundation, and I asked that she stop by the nursery after dropping off the mower and buy the plants. That way I could jump right on getting them all planted when I came the following Saturday. My last request was that she try to make some progress on the trim painting in the house. She said she could do all of this, and I'd headed back to my office for the night, telling her I'd see her the next Saturday.

When Saturday came and I pulled my little Z3 to a stop in front of the house, I was not happy. The mower was right where I'd left it, and there were no bushes in sight.

I asked if the mower was repaired, and she said "You know I can't get it loaded in that trailer by myself!" I wasn't sure what was so hard about driving it up the ramp, or why she'd agreed to something that she had no intention of doing.

Then I asked her about the bushes, and she said, "Oh, you know what you want more than I do, let's just go now. Better yet, why don't you go and I'll stay here and get other things done."

So I went to the nursery at 10 a.m. on a fall Saturday, and it was packed. Two hours later, I was back with a trailer load of plants. I spent the afternoon planting four trees, twelve bushes and ten decorative grasses, while Jenny planted a row of Mondo grass. I was starting with the sun high in the sky, and by the time I finished the long sweaty job, it was early evening. I walked into the house, and was not surprised to see that no trim painting had been done.

Ever since Jenny had asked for a separation, I'd spent many sleepless nights at my desk in front of the moonlit window of my study, gazing out at the barn and pasture, wondering how to repair things between us. Many letters had been written to her in those nights, declaring my love and asking her to try again, to not throw away the 27 years of memories we had together. Now I asked her if she'd given any thought to my last letter. I'd written her about what I thought needed to change for us to get back together, and I'd been asking for a response. She'd been avoiding discussing it, but she agreed to get the letter and talk about it. We sat on the back porch as she settled in with her wine and cigarettes.

I told her the first point in my letter was "Promise you won't do this again. Agree that this time it's really forever, like you promised 27 years ago."

She replied that "There are no guarantees in life."

I asked again, saying "I'm not asking for a promise that we'll never have problems, just that you won't use divorce as a solution every time we have a disagreement."

She declined, saying again "There are no guarantees in life." That was a pretty big problem, but I went to the next point

"Do what you say you will. Follow through, and if you don't get something done, don't blame me for it."

She asked me for an example, and I knew we were on dangerous ground with her temper. I pointed out that she'd agreed to get three things done in the last seven days to help with the sale of the house, and she hadn't done any of them. I gave her the examples, the mower repair, the bushes and the painting, and the fact the she blamed me for expecting her to do it in the first place.

She jumped out of her chair, yelled at me that "You are ridiculous, I just can't talk to you anymore!" and stormed off of the porch.

I sat there in frustration for a minute, then followed her into the kitchen, where she had started washing dishes. There was an interior pass through window over the kitchen sink, and she kept her head down and tried not to look at me as I said "Jenny, how are we ever going to fix this if we can't even talk about it without you storming off?"

She started yelling at me to just "Leave me alone!"

I said again "We've got to be able to talk!"

With that she shrieked at me at the top of her lungs to "GET THE F**K OUT!"

I was stunned and angry that she would talk to me like that, and I told her "If I leave now, I won't be coming back."

She screamed at me again, and I told her I wouldn't be back. Jenny knew that unlike her, I always do what I say I will. I got in my car, gravel spinning off the tires as I blasted out of the driveway, and drove back to the studio. I walked into the huge open space, stood under the dome and took off my wedding band for the first time in 27 years. I mourned the end of our marriage, but to me a line had been crossed. I was done.

Epilogue
Fall 2001

It was over. When a friend came to the studio the following day, he looked at me as I came bounding down the stairs from my office to greet him.

He stopped me half way down and said "What happened, you look different?" I wasn't sure what he meant, until he said "I know what it is. You look happy!"

And he was right. I'd spent the past 27 years fighting a losing battle to make Jenny a happy and fulfilled person, but the struggle was over. I felt like the weight of the world had been lifted from my shoulders, and the future looked hopeful. The stress of fighting separation over the past five months had put a strain on me that was noticeable to my friends and family, and now it was over. I could smile again.

In many ways the two week trip on the Waxing Gibbous

down the Intra Coastal Waterway had given me a new perspective on my time with Jenny. Telling Captain Rick the story of my life and career had set it all out in front of me in a way that many people never experience until the end of their lives. I'd loved Jenny, encouraged her, pushed her to find what she wanted out of life. But my love hadn't been enough. One of my many letters to her said "I spent 27 years trying to help you overcome your demons, and now you've decided I'm one of them." That may have been the greatest hurt of all. With all of her problems, the thing that had always bound us together was love. I had to believe she loved me. I'm sure my inability to understand why she did the things she did contributed to our marital struggles, but I always loved her and wanted the best for her.

During the five months I fought against separation at the farm, I told her how hard her scorn had been to take in recent months. When finances became stretched and I had to start refusing her requests for more "things", she characterized me as mean. It didn't matter that we couldn't afford things because of a dip in the economy.

I was simply mean for refusing her.

One day at the farm I said to her "Jenny, my family thinks I'm a nice guy. My friends think I'm a nice guy. My employees and clients all think I'm a nice guy. The only person who seems to think I'm terrible is you. Do you know how hurtful that is?" Her reply stunned me.

"They don't know you like I do."

Keeping Us Afloat

As painful as the growing realization that my wife didn't love me anymore was for me, coming to the end of my 27 years of struggling with her demons was a relief. I've always been a person who embraced change, who looked on every day as being filled with possibilities. The one thing I couldn't do was make Jenny a happy person. Now it was no longer my job, it would be up to her.

There were a lot of difficult moments yet to come, but I finally felt in control of my own destiny. The only person I had to make happy was me.

A week after the blowup, I needed Jenny one last time. On September 11th, I was watching the news on TV as the announcer discussed a plane hitting the World Trade Center. At that early report, it was believed to be an accident. I was heading next door for a massage, a trade on a reduction of the rent for the apartment beside the studio that I received every two weeks. When I came back an hour later, the second plane had hit and the first tower had fallen. As my staff and I watched in horror, the second tower fell. We tried to work that day, but it was difficult.

When I started getting a pain in my side near lunch time, I wasn't sure what it was at first. When it turned into piercing agony, my friend and co-worker George rushed me to the doctor. The doctor quickly diagnosed kidney stones, and sent me to the nearest hospital. For anyone that's ever had them, no explanation is necessary. For those who haven't, I've a friend who has had two children and also had kidney stones. She says the kidney stones are "much worse than labor pains." The doctors didn't feel I was a candidate for lithotripsy to break the stones up, and sent me home with a large amount of morphine to get me through the excruciating pain. My staff had called Jenny, and she showed up at the hospital and agreed to take me home to pass the stones.

Over the next three days, while the world watched endless replays of the planes hitting the towers, I lay semi conscious in the bedroom of the farmhouse. Every time I started to wake up, the intense pain washed over me and Jenny brought more morphine. By the time the pain subsided three days later and I was awake enough to look at the television, the networks had decided the endless replays of the planes hitting the towers was too traumatic, and they quit showing them. Coverage was still intense, but 9/11 has always had an unreal quality for me because I missed so much of it.

After a few more days I'd recovered, and Jenny and I parted ways pretty much for good. We had one more evening together, when I took her to a Tori Amos concert in early October at the Fox Theatre in Atlanta for our 27th anniversary, but the time together was tinged with sadness. We both knew it was over. I gave her a final anniversary plaque, one that declared I would always be her friend if she wanted me to be. The plaques had seemed so unimportant to her for many years, but she acted disappointed by the message. She had told her mother that she wondered if there would even be a plaque that year.

The next year would bring a painful and expensive divorce, but my life felt like it was starting anew. As my friends and family asked what had happened with my marriage to Jenny and I relayed stories of my life with her and her demands over the previous 27 years, it was like awakening from a spell. The more I told others about our relationship, the crazier it sounded to me. It reminded me of my last day driving the bread truck in college. The more I had described to my helper that day about what the job entailed, the more I wondered why I was doing it. It was much the same with the breakup with Jenny. I can't imagine why I put up with that all those years. Call it Love, or maybe just keeping my "Till death do us part" vow, I'd never been willing to give up on us. Then she took the decision away from me, and I was grateful.

In all of the years Jenny and I had been together I'd wanted her to be happy; to feel the joy in life that I felt every day; to see possibilities instead of problems; to know the excitement that every day has the potential to bring. But it just wasn't in her.

I'd accepted it as my duty to bring her that happiness, and only at the end realized that it could only come from within her. I believe happiness is a decision we all have to make, to enjoy what you have, not mourn what you don't. I was trying to fill a need for her that only she could fill for herself, so of course I failed. Life was now ahead of me again, and I only had myself to keep afloat.

For a few months I avoided socializing, spending lots of

evenings with friends, commiserating over being suddenly middle-aged and single. I settled into my bachelor quarters at the studio, with Jenny and I limiting our communications to phone calls about selling the farm and divorce settlements. It was strange, as we'd spoken every day for more than a quarter century. Now we spoke maybe once a week, and not about personal things. It was what she wanted.

Many times I'd spend the night at friend's houses, happy for the company but feeling the awkwardness that comes with being single with couple friends. In the following spring I told Jenny I was going to start dating, and she replied "You can't do that, you're a married man!"

I found that ironic, since she was the one who didn't want to be married. A No Fault divorce in South Carolina required a one year separation period, and we were just waiting for the time to be up. That's not what I consider being married.

I'd never dated much, having kept the same girlfriend through the last two years of high school and the first year of college, and then marrying Jenny when I was just 21 years old. Now I was finally ready to venture out again. I had been on a few dates, telling them all that I was not interested in starting a relationship, just in enjoying each other's company. One of my New Years resolutions was 'No entanglements'. I didn't want an exclusive relationship, and didn't date anyone who wanted to have one.

I wasn't thinking marriage, just fun and companionship.

And then I met Marilyn.

But that's another story.

David Crosby

There are many people who've made a difference in my life, and I'd like to thank a few of them.

First and foremost my parents, Hubert and Mary Crosby. I got my love of travel from my Mom, my work ethic from my Dad and my sense of right and wrong from them both. Growing up knowing your parents will always love you and believe in you is a gift I've always treasured. They also gave me the feeling that I could do anything I wanted to, if I just tried hard enough.

My brother and sister and the extended family of cousins and grandparents that filled my childhood with Love.

My first grade friend Robert Tippett was my first exposure to art with his love of photography, poetry and writing. And we're still friends.

During the many years of my photography studio my employees and friends George Reynolds and Kelly Brogdon shared the work and the travel, and always made it fun. You are both treasured friends.

Charlie and Mona Register, friends for more than 30 years, thank you for being there when my life felt like it was falling apart. You gave me a place to recover and pick up the pieces.

And most of all to my incredible wife Marilyn. You gave me the love and romance that I dreamed of as a child, and you took my hand and traveled the world with me.

You also gave me children and grandchildren, a dream I'd long since given up on.

I love you Sweetie.

Thanks to all of my readers, and I will be eternally grateful for any of you who take the time to post a short review on the Amazon page for this book.

David Crosby
Greenville, SC
October
2013

About the Author

David Crosby grew up in Atlanta, Georgia, making weekly trips to the library with his Dad. David's love of reading became a love of imagination and creativity, which he finally found an outlet for in college at the University of Georgia.

David received an ABJ degree in magazine writing from the UGA School of Journalism, but it was his newly discovered interest in photography that took over his working life.

Starting at graduation, Crosby spent nearly eight years as a photojournalist for newspapers before a desire for self-employment led him to try his hand at commercial photography.

David has run Crosby Stills, his award winning commercial studio for the past 28 years, and lives in Greenville with his wife Marilyn, a Lutheran Pastor.

David Crosby can be reached at david@crosbystills.com.

Keeping Us Afloat